GREAT GIFTS
YOU CAN MAKE IN MINUTES

BETH FRANKS

Cincinnati, OH

About the Author

Since her first batiking project in grade school, Beth Franks has been involved in a variety of art forms—from papier mache to theatre. As an adult she has created her own presents for many gift-giving occasions. The artist/author writes for several magazines; her "Great Gift Ideas" column appears in the *Decorative Artist's Workbook*. This is her fifth book.

Great Gifts You Can Make in Minutes

Copyright © 1992 by Beth Franks. Printed and bound in the United States of America. All rights reserved. No part of this book may be reproduced in any form or by any electronic or mechanical means including information storage and retrieval systems without permission in writing from the publisher, except by a reviewer, who may quote brief passages in a review. Published by North Light Books, an imprint of F&W Publications, Inc., 1507 Dana Avenue, Cincinnati, Ohio 45207; 1(800)289-0963. First Edition.

96 95 94 93 92   5 4 3 2 1

Note: Every effort has been made to ensure that all the information in this book is accurate. However, due to differing conditions, tools, and individual skills, the author and publisher cannot be responsible for any injuries, losses, or other damages which may result from the use of the information in this book.

Library of Congress Cataloging in Publication Data
Franks, Beth.
   Great gifts you can make in minutes / Beth Franks. — 1st ed.
      p.   cm.
   Includes index.
   ISBN 0-89134-432-2 (paper)
   1. Handicraft. 2. Cookery. 3. Gifts. I. Title.
   TT157.F73   1992   92-14780
   745.5—dc20   CIP

Edited by Sandra Carpenter
Designed by Clare Finney
Illustrations by Cathryn Cunningham
Photography by Pamela Monfort

A gift, though small, is precious.
— Homer

Acknowledgments

Publishing is a collaborative enterprise — many people helped make this book a reality. I'd especially like to thank the following people: Sandy Carpenter, my editor, who offered valuable suggestions, polished my prose, and provided encouragement throughout the writing and editing process; photographer and stylist extraordinaire, Pam Monfort, who took the color pictures that will inspire you to create; and Cathy Cunningham, who drew the illustrations and chapter openers that grace these pages.

I'm also grateful to the talented women who contributed their craft projects to be photographed: Laura Bolt, Maya Contento, Debbie Vitkow Davidson, Tari Sasser Jacober, Patty Knapp and her sister Barbara Brown, Linda Konowal and Ann McSwiggin. In addition, I'm indebted to Myra Griffin, Gladys Dood, Gloria Esenwein, Barbara Brady and Martha Vieth Petry for sharing their recipes. Thanks also go to the staffs of the Lavender Stick Flower Shop in Milford, Ohio, and of Reminiscent Herb Farm in Florence, Kentucky, for putting me in touch with resources.

Bill Brohaugh and David Lewis, Editorial Directors of Writer's Digest Books and North Light Books respectively, helped get this idea off the ground, while Mike Ward, editor of *The Artist's Magazine*, gave me the opportunity to develop lots of projects in the pages of a special magazine, *101 Gift Ideas*. Mert Ransdell made the negotiation process painless, Mary Junewick shepherded the manuscript through production, and Christy Pretzinger and Sue Ann Stein helped out with marketing. All deserve a hearty "Thank You!"

Last but not least, thanks to Michael, who gives me inspiration and support through all my creative endeavors.

TABLE OF CONTENTS

ONE

THE SEARCH FOR THE PERFECT GIFT

*H*ow many millions of dollars have been wasted on gifts that end up in the back of the closet or in some far corner of the basement? Given with the best intentions, these things just don't suit the recipient—he or she has no need for this gift, doesn't want it, it's the wrong style, color, size or is somehow just not right.

It's true that ideas are the hardest part—to find "the perfect gift" you must give some thought to a specific individual. That's why on page 3 you'll find a questionnaire to help with the brainstorming process. And once you hit upon a good idea for a present, making it yourself virtually guarantees success. Plus, it can be more rewarding for you. Here's why:

•*You give the gift of yourself.* There's something special about a handcrafted gift; when tailor-made for a special person, an object gains a certain power. Ralph Waldo Emerson said, "The only gift is a portion of thyself." Because there's something of the person who crafted it in even the smallest handmade gift, it becomes "the only gift."

•*It's original.* A one-of-a-kind personalized gift communicates love and caring in a way that store-bought gifts cannot.

•*Handmade gifts are made to be cherished.* They can even become future heirlooms. Just think, the basket you decorate today could hold your great-granddaughter's knitting supplies; a hand-painted picture frame may someday house the photo of a baby born in 2091.

•*You save time.* Keep in mind that making a gift doesn't necessarily take more time than shopping for one. Consider that you must drive to the mall or store, look around for a suitable gift, perhaps agonize over your decision, stand in line, purchase it, then drive home. Many wonderful handmade gifts can be put together in minutes.

•*You save money.* Another bonus is that you can make something yourself for a small fraction of what it would cost to buy a comparable gift. Case in point: I saw a pinecone basket in a department store last Christmas that had a price tag of twenty-five dollars. I was able to make an identical basket (see page 16) using a plain basket, some hot glue sticks, and pinecones I gathered myself. It was more personal. And, best of all, my basket cost less than five dollars!

•*It's something for you, too.* Because it is better to give than to receive, you're not only giving a gift to another person, but to yourself as well. Making something beautiful with your own hands provides a wonderful feeling of satisfaction and a boost to your self-esteem. The act of creation can be stimulating or relaxing, but it's rarely dull.

DO-IT-YOURSELF GIFTS

In this book, you'll discover how to make elegant, yet inexpensive, gifts for everyone on your list. Ideas range from homemade potpourri and pomanders to painted T-shirts, rag rugs, and one-of-a-kind gift baskets—you'll even find instructions for making your own wrapping paper.

Some gifts are simple to put together and can be completed in less than an hour, while others require a bit more time (gifts that require painting, for example, will need time for drying), but all are suitable for beginners. Many of the ideas can be varied according to how much energy you want to expend—you could decorate pillowcases with tie-dye or potato printing, for instance, for totally different looks. You could make earrings out of paper, fish lures, fossils or feathers. You might use dried flowers of the same types to make a variety of gifts—a wreath, a swag, a bouquet or a topiary—depending on the person, and how much time you have available.

You'll find this book is a good source for ideas as well as a handy how-to-do-it guide. Each of the following chapters includes an Ideas section. These ideas can be adapted using a variety of techniques, so you can tailor-make a gift for an individual. The How-To section that follows each Ideas section provides step-by-step instructions for the techniques described.

Even if you maintain you "aren't creative," there are ideas in this book for you, too. Making things yourself often consists largely of assembling materials you already have on hand. Take the pinecone basket described before. All it took was a basket, a glue gun, some pinecones and an idea (that I copied from something I saw in a department store). Anybody can do it! All you really need is the desire, a good idea, and some initiative. Chapter Two, which features gift baskets, is a good place to start if you're somewhat intimidated by the creative process. Then page through the rest of the book, and you'll find many ideas that are quick and easy to make, no matter what your crafting experience.

Ideas Are the Key

Asking the right questions is the answer to finding the perfect gift. Each person has a different profile, different needs and wants, and different tastes. Think about what a person likes to do in his or her spare time. Think about home furnishings — colors, textures, shapes. What kinds of decorations are on the wall? Does this person already own handmade things and display them prominently? What about clothing? What colors and styles does this person wear?

Whether you purchase a gift or make it yourself, this question-and-answer process is the most important part of gift-giving. You need to put yourself in the shoes of the recipient. Life-styles differ, and the perfect gift for your mother may be all wrong for your aunt. Handmade gifts, unfortunately, are not foolproof. Unlike doting parents who cherish everything their offspring creates, other people are not so indulgent.

Some handmade gifts are "safer" than others.

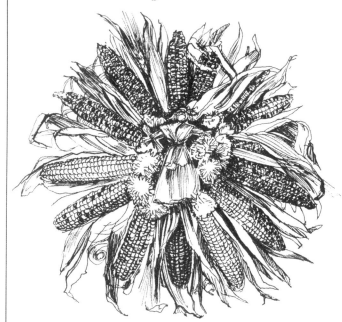

Often, the time of year may suggest a gift idea. This Indian corn wreath, with dried strawflowers and a corn husk doll in the center, makes a perfect autumn gift for someone who likes to decorate her home seasonally. (See Chapter Two for more wreath ideas.)

Food is almost universally appreciated, unless the person is dieting (as more and more people seem to be). Gift baskets are a traditionally "safe" gift; they can make a powerful statement, especially when they're personalized. Again, the key is giving careful thought to the specific person.

Because too often the hardest part of gift-giving is deciding *what* to give, I've provided a Gift Profile questionnaire to help you answer this key question for each person on your list. An easy reference guide will then lead you to the chapters in this book that have the "best bets" for each person.

THE GIFT PROFILE

The Gift Profile was designed to stimulate your brainstorming process. Simply make enough photocopies of the form (or use blank sheets of paper) so you have one for each person on your list, then write out the answers to the questions for each person. If you don't know someone well enough to answer a question, be alert for clues whenever you spend time with him or her. It may seem like a lot of work now, but it will pay off for years to come. Keep completed profiles in a file and update them as you gain more information. Be sure to note which gifts seem to be most successful with each person!

Best Bets

Check your answers to the Gift Profile against the suggestions in this section. This will help direct you to the "best bets" for each person.

1. If you've already seen how this person reacts to different gifts, you've got a big head start. Write those gifts you're sure were pleasers in the blank at the top of the profile, and use them as a guide in your brainstorming process.

2. Knowing what a person does in his or her spare time can be a big help in finding the perfect gift. If someone likes to read, you could give her a beautiful bookmark, whereas an athletic type would prefer a set of colorful sweatbands. Because of the range of options here, any of the chapters in this book may hold possibilities. Keep this information in mind as you review the rest of the list.

3. Likewise, a person's hobby can help you zero in on what he or she likes. A woman who paints would appreciate a box for her supplies (see Chapter Six);

THE GIFT PROFILE

Name _____

Birthday _____

Favorite gifts (if known) _____

_____

1. If you have past experience in gift-giving situations with this person, which gifts seem to make him or her most excited? Least excited?

_____

_____

2. What does this person enjoy doing in his or her spare time? (For instance, consider whether this person would rather be reading or playing sports.)

_____

_____

3. Does he or she have a hobby? What is it?

_____

_____

4. What is this person's favorite color?

_____

5. Has this person expressed a need or desire for anything lately? ("I wish I had time to play more tennis." Or, "I saw the greatest dress downtown!")

_____

_____

6. Does this person enjoy eating? What is this person's favorite food? Does he or she have a sweet tooth?

_____

_____

7. How does this person relate to the natural world? Does he or she like to garden? Camp? Hike?

_____

_____

8. How does this person dress? In the latest fashions, or jeans and a sweatshirt? Would you characterize his or her style as preppy or funky? Formal or casual? What size does this person wear?

_____

_____

_____

9. Does this person wear jewelry? If so, what kind? Earrings, rings, bracelets, necklaces?

_____

_____

10. Does this person have a home office?

_____

11. Does this person enjoy decorating?

_____

12. How would you characterize this person's style? Frilly, rugged, modern, traditional, country, urban, romantic and eclectic are a few examples.

_____

_____

_____

13. Does this person have a passion for something? Some people love owls or elephants, others are teddy bear freaks. Similarly, is there a specific place, or area of the country, that this person is partial to?

_____

_____

_____

14. Is this a person who says they don't want anything?

_____

_____

a cook might enjoy a gourmet wreath (see Chapter Three); and a shutterbug might like a custom album for displaying snapshots (see Chapter Four). Again, the possibilities are nearly endless, but your specific answers should help guide you to the appropriate chapter.

4. Knowing a person's favorite color will help you no matter what gift you decide on, because you can apply it to any medium: dried flower arrangements, wreaths, clothing, jewelry, notepads, pillows, place mats, even baskets.

5. If she admired your safety pin bracelet, this is an obvious choice for a gift (see Chapter Six for this and other jewelry ideas). If she complains she has nothing to wear, give her a beautifully decorated T-shirt or silk scarf (see Chapter Four). Gift baskets, discussed in Chapter Two, encompass a lot of "wish list" items. Always keep your ears open for hints dropped unwittingly in casual conversation.

6. Anyone who likes to eat appreciates a gift of food. Chapter Five has lots of delicious recipes for sweets and healthy treats as well.

7. Many people who like the out-of-doors like to surround themselves with reminders of the natural world. See Chapter Three, Gifts from the Garden, and consider those ideas in Chapter Six that use found materials, such as seashells, rocks and fossils.

8. Clothes always make a great gift, as long as they suit the person's style—and they're the right size! A fashionable woman might appreciate a hand-painted silk scarf, or even a potato-printed T-shirt. Someone who wears jeans all the time might like an appliquéd sweatshirt (see Chapter Four). For the wild and crazy dressers, consider a pair of hand-painted tennis shoes (see Chapter Six).

9. Taste in jewelry, like that in clothes, varies incredibly from person to person. A woman with a taste for the exotic might like a pair of feather earrings, while a more conservative type would prefer a button pin (see Chapter Six).

10. People with home offices often appreciate things for their desks—pencil holders, blotters and letter baskets. (See Chapters Four and Seven). In addition, there are suggestions in Chapter Two for several gift baskets tailor-made for business types.

11. People who enjoy decorating are sometimes persnickety, but if you get the color and style right,

gifts for the home make a big impact. Consider pillows, wall hangings and table accessories (Chapter Four), as well as decorations made of dried plants (Chapter Three).

12. If you answered yes to number eleven, this information will help you design the perfect gift.

13. When someone has a passion for something, you usually can't go wrong if you incorporate it into the gift. While an owl pillow or a tablecloth appliquéd with a border of elephants might leave the average person cold, they'll score with people who are enamored with those creatures. Use your imagination when thinking of ways to apply the fetish to a gift. (This can also be expanded beyond specifics to more general themes: a seashell mirror for someone who loves the beach, for instance.)

14. Sometimes people who say they don't want anything are simply self-effacing and don't want others to be bothered for them. Others don't want gifts because they feel obligated to reciprocate. Another possibility is that this person is tired of getting gifts that don't suit her. And some people may actually "have it all," and not want a gift. If possible, determine which group this person belongs to.

•For the self-effacing: Simply ignore their protests and let the answers to the other questions guide you to the "best bet" for this person.

•For the obligated: Give a small gift (see Chapter Six), or a gift of food (see Chapter Five).

•For the disenchanted: Pay special attention to this person's style, choice of colors for clothes and home furnishings, and listen for clues of what he or she *does* like. Use the answers to the other questions on this survey to help you satisfy a hard-to-please person. (Also see the suggestions under the next category and in the Other Gift Ideas section that follows.)

•For those who have it all: Even people who have everything need to eat. Why not hold a dinner party with this person as the guest of honor? (See Chapter Five for menus and recipes.)

Other Gift Ideas
You'll find gift ideas are everywhere—in magazines, books, shops, friends' homes. But sometimes an object doesn't mean half as much as an action—the proverbial "thought that counts." For instance, a new mother just home from the hospital might appreciate

a door-to-door delivery of lunch more than a basket full of baby lotions and powder. Someone who complains they never see you anymore would probably prefer spending time with you for an evening rather than getting a present in the mail. Be sensitive to other people's needs, and give accordingly.

Also remember that you don't have to make gifts for everybody on your list. Some people are really tough to figure out, so rather than guess at something, why not go with a sure thing? The following list contains some ideas for the people who have you stumped.

• Gift certificates to movies, restaurants, department stores, book shops, car washes, dry cleaners, etc.

• Subscriptions to magazines and newspapers relating to a person's interests.

• Annual memberships to museums, symphonies, ballets, or an automobile club.

• Personalized gift certificates, "Good for one fishing trip," or "Good for one week of dishwashing."

• A dinner party or a luncheon as a gift.

• For kids who like to be read to, make audio tapes of their favorite stories. If they're learning to read on their own, tape yourself reading their favorite book; tap a knife against a glass to make a tone that will be a signal to turn the page.

• "A Thought a Day": Collect 365 inspiring quotes, type them up, then photocopy them. Cut the sayings apart, then place them in a pretty glass jar. The recipient can then pull one a day from the jar.

• Family history: If you have access to old family documents and photos, this can make a great gift for relatives. Gather your source materials together and photocopy them; have duplicates made of old photographs. Put them in a loose-leaf notebook and give to family members. A related idea is a personal history. The mother of a friend of mine put together a book of old school papers, crayoned pictures and handmade cards she'd saved through the years. My friend was touched by the fact that her mother had saved her "artwork," and enjoyed having these momentos of her younger self.

GET ORGANIZED FOR GIFT-GIVING

To help streamline the giving process, professional organizers recommend you set aside an area in your house devoted solely to gift wrapping. A corner of the basement or the spare room is ideal; if you have a room or area set aside for crafting, this is an obvious choice. (See the section on Setting Up Your Work Space later in this chapter.) If you live in an apartment, you may only have room for a box in the corner of a closet, or even under the bed, for storing completed gifts and wrapping supplies, but set aside some small area nonetheless. Some people use cedar chests or footlockers for this purpose. In this "gift center," keep everything associated with wrapping: paper, ribbon, tape, cards, a special set of scissors (used only in this area—never removed!), colored pens, mailing tape and brown mailing paper, as well as your cache of gifts. You may also want to keep your Gift Profiles with this stuff, though I like to keep mine near my desk so I can add to them easily. Ideally, you'll be able to wrap gifts near your gift center. But if this is not possible, when it is time to wrap, move your supplies to the dining room table or other handy spot.

Some people like to wrap gifts ahead of time, especially if they have nosey children (or a curious spouse) and want to keep gifts a surprise. If you opt to wrap ahead, be sure to label gifts clearly with the intended recipient's name to avoid confusion later!

Once you've set aside a "gift center," give some thought to your calendar of gift-giving. We'll deal with that gift extravaganza, Christmas, in a minute, but for now think about birthdays, anniversaries, graduations, Mother's and Father's Days, showers and weddings.

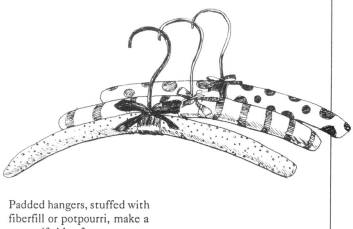

Padded hangers, stuffed with fiberfill or potpourri, make a great gift idea for someone who loves clothes. (See Chapter Four for how to make hangers.)

Take twelve sheets of paper and write the names of the month on each, then list in order dates you know to be important, for example, "October: 9th, Judy's birthday; 18th, Susie's birthday; 19th, Chris's birthday." Then, at the beginning of each month, transfer these dates to your calendar so you'll remember to send a card, if not a gift, to help commemorate each person's special day.

If you're especially organized—or a consummate gift-giver—consider investing in a Book of Days, a calendar that lists the dates of the months without mentioning the days of the week, so it's good from year to year. Write all your important gift-giving occasions in there and keep it forever. The only trick to this method is remembering to look at your Book of Days! If you're forgetful, you may still want to transfer important dates to your current monthly calendar to ensure they aren't overlooked.

Avoiding the Christmas Crazies

For years my dad made stained glass and sold it in local shops and at fairs, and every year he witnessed something he called "the Christmas crazies." As the holidays approached, he found people would buy things they'd never consider at any other time of year. "I'll take two!" they'd cry frantically. Dad was always glad to make the sale, of course, but he felt a little sorry for these folks, with their wild eyes and their thinly disguised desperation.

Conversely, last June, my incredibly organized friend Lita said to me, "Christmas is getting close!" This attitude is important if you intend to make all your gifts. You've got to get some projects out of the way ahead of time if you want to maintain your sanity during the holidays.

Start by making a list of everyone you want to give gifts to this Christmas. Include everybody—your neighbors, coworkers, your daughter's Girl Scout leader, the paperboy—it doesn't matter how simple you think it will be to take care of these people, put them on your list! (Last minute gifts for people you've overlooked can wreak havoc with your schedule.) Begin brainstorming now for ideas for each person, and as you discover pretty good bets, write them down. Keep a piece of paper beside you as you read this book, and jot down ideas as you get them. You may think you'll remember, but if you're like most

people, there's lots on your mind, and ideas have a way of moving on. I keep a small notepad with me at all times to write down gift ideas for specific people as well as nifty items I see when I'm shopping or visiting friends.

Although next Christmas is probably the last thing on your mind in January, this can actually be an ideal time to start brainstorming for gift ideas; people's reactions to Christmas gifts will be fresh in your mind. I keep a piece of paper in the front of my Gift File listing everybody I want to give to, with several ideas by each name. You don't have to complete your list right away, but get to work on it and you'll save yourself a lot of anguish later.

As you settle on ideas for different people, begin making some of those gifts and stash them in a suitcase or a box in a closet. If possible, batch projects according to type. For instance, if you're going to make potato-printed place mats for Aunt Louise, and a potato-printed T-shirt for your sister, it makes sense to do these projects at the same time, while you're all set up for potato printing. Likewise, I often make duplicate items of easy gifts like earrings and notepads, even if I have no one in mind to give them to. That way, when unexpected gift-giving situations arise, I'm prepared and don't have to scramble.

Setting Up Your Work Space

To make your own gifts you'll need a well-lighted area in which to work, as well as a few basic supplies. If you have a basement or a spare bedroom, you can convert either of these into a craft studio. Sometimes a sewing area can be expanded to incorporate crafts as well. With a room set up permanently for crafts, you can create on a moment's notice, and simply close the door if you have to leave something in process. Your supplies will be ready when you need them.

If you have only a corner of a room available, use a nearby cupboard or chest of drawers to corral all your projects and supplies when you aren't crafting. A card table can be set up nearby when you're ready to work. If you have extra cupboard space in the kitchen in which to store supplies, this room might make a good makeshift studio. I lived in one-bedroom apartments for more than a decade and made gifts on the dining room table; all my supplies were stored in plastic crates in the hall closet. (Keepers, from Rubbermaid, are the best I've found—they have lids that fasten, come in a wide range of sizes and a variety of bright, cheerful colors.) Every time I wanted to make something, I pulled out the crates, set up a card table beside the dining table to expand my work surface, and transformed the room into a studio. Now I live in a house and have a permanent workroom in the basement, making life a lot easier. I'm glad I had the experience of "making do," however, because I can honestly testify it can be done! No matter what your circumstances, with a little thought, you can set up a comfortable work area in which to create great gifts.

Basic Supplies

As you compile your gift list, keep a separate shopping list of supplies you'll need to buy. Once you sit down to work, you'll want to avoid running out to the store to pick up forgotten items, so keep this list diligently! If you're super-organized and complete your entire list before you begin making the gifts, you may be able to buy all your supplies at once, thus saving a lot of time. In any case, always try to buy materials for a minimum of three gifts whenever you go to the craft store; this will increase your efficiency and allow you more time to create.

The following list is included as a guideline. Not every project will require all of these supplies. For most projects, you'll probably need a few additional items, but this is a good, basic list of things to have on hand. Check it against individual projects you intend to make before purchasing anything.

Scrap paper	Hammer and nails
Paper towels	Wire cutters
Colored tissue paper	Masking tape
Construction paper	White glue
Newspapers	Hot glue gun
Cardboard	Water-based varnish
Old magazines	or shellac
Pencils	Paintbrushes
Ruler	Acrylic paints
Scissors	Fabric paints
X-Acto knife	Florist wire

Fusible web	Old junk jewelry
Fabric scraps	Pinecones
Needle and thread	Palette (or an old
Straight pins	plate)
Ribbon	Empty bottles
Poly-fil foam	Coffee cans
Jewelry findings	Styrofoam meat trays
Beads	

THE GIFT OF YOURSELF

You'll find hundreds of gift ideas in the following pages, which may trigger even more possibilities in your mind. As a firm believer in brainstorming, I'm convinced that ideas are endless—all we have to do is let them in. By focusing on specific individuals and letting your mind roam, you're sure to come up with a perfect gift idea every time.

People are thrilled to get one-of-a-kind gifts, especially ones that represent an investment of time and care on your part. I hope that by using the ideas in this book, you'll be proud to say "I made it myself."

A log cabin planter has a rustic appeal that many folks find irresistible. You can also use this simple style of construction to make an end table. See Chapter Three for instructions.

TWO

GIFT BASKETS
FOR EVERY OCCASION

*G*ift baskets are a great way to get creative without actually having to make anything. They're often composed entirely of things you've purchased, but because you chose each item with the recipient in mind, the overall effect is very personal—as it is with all handmade gifts. Unless you decide to paint them, gift baskets usually take only an hour (or less) to complete, so they can work well at the last minute. All you need is a good idea.

Ideas for baskets fall into two basic categories: specific holidays, such as Easter, and themes, such as bath or gourmet baskets. In the next section you'll find lots of suggestions for both types of baskets, but begin by focusing on the person for whom the gift is intended. Use the checklist in Chapter One to help define the recipient's tastes and preferences, then brainstorm possibilities based on everything you know about this individual.

For instance, let's say George adores his vintage Porsche. He's also a Cubs fan, and he likes to bicycle. At first glance, he's not a very good candidate for a gift basket. But consider a "Car Lover's Basket," filled with car care supplies, or an "Emergency Basket," containing things like a flashlight, flares and jumper cables to be kept in the trunk of his Porsche; or what about a "Sports Lover's Basket," with Cubs memorabilia, or a "Bicyclist's Basket"? All at once, you have four great gift ideas for George.

All of the baskets I just mentioned are in the Ideas section of this chapter, but you might decide to create a special "Porsche Basket" just for George. Find a Porsche key ring, an "I love my Porsche" bumper sticker, a Matchbox toy Porsche, a book on Porsches, some car wax, chamois and a pair of sporty sunglasses, then put them in a basket you've painted with green enamel, the exact same color as his car. Make a greeting card using a picture of a car cut from a magazine or a photo of his car, and the gift is complete. It's perfect for George.

This example brings up another important point: It's a snap to decorate a basket yourself. With a couple of coats of green enamel, you created a tailor-made Porsche basket, and you can choose from a vast array of paint colors on the market to assure that your other gift baskets will be unique. Dilute the paint for a "pickled" effect, brush dark paint over a white base

coat for an antiqued look (rub off most of the paint before it dries for a soft tint), or use some of the specific products designed for special effects on wood to create a one-of-a-kind basket.

Besides paint, there are lots more quick and easy ways to personalize a ready-made basket. You can use fabric, ribbons, dried or silk flowers, buttons, beads, lace, pine cones, novelty items—whatever you dream up. By the time you finish decorating it, the basket may be a gift in itself. (For more details on these possibilities, see the How-To section later in this chapter.)

If you're willing to invest a substantial amount of time, you could even make the basket yourself. For more information, check out *The Basket Book: Over 30 Magnificent Baskets to Make and Enjoy*, by Lyn Siler (Sterling Publishing Co.).

But you don't have to limit yourself to a basket. Vary the theme and give a dieting friend a "Salad Basket," filled with herbed croutons, gourmet vinegar, olive oil, low sodium herbal seasoning, cloves of garlic, and green, yellow and red peppers—all presented in a wooden bowl. Or give a unique "Gardener's Basket," as described in the following section, but use a large, dried, hollowed-out gourd as a container.

The simplest gift baskets are built around a single item or class of items. For example, a mustard basket might include mustard chutney, Dijon mustard, Cajun mustard and dry mustard; an Italian food basket could be filled with pasta, tomato sauces, pepperoni, olive oil, Romano cheese, and herbs such as basil, oregano and garlic.

You can also make small gifts that will work in a variety of different baskets—things like sachets, potholders, magnets, decorated jars, jewelry and bouquets of dried flowers. There are lots of ideas throughout this book, and you'll come up with plenty of your own if you let your imagination roam.

IDEAS

The following list of both thematic and holiday gift basket ideas will get you started. Just remember that you may come up with an even better idea via brainstorming, so don't limit yourself to my suggestions.

Gourmet Basket: To begin, find a big basket with a handle. Line it with a decorative cloth and fill it with cheeses, crackers, preserves, honey, exotic condiments, herbs and spices, herbal vinegar, salami, coffee, tea, chocolates, cookies, fruits, nuts, liqueurs and wine or sparkling cider. Use a plain basket, or decorate it with paint, fabric or just a big bow. If you want to go all out, include a set of hand-printed napkins and place mats as I did for the basket pictured on page 12. (See Chapter Four for more ideas on fabric decoration.) Also, remember that any one of these items could form the basis for an entire basket. A gourmet vinegar basket, for instance, could include apple cider and wine vinegars, as well as tarragon, garlic and malt vinegars; a nut basket might be filled with shelled and unshelled Brazils, pecans, walnuts, sunflower seeds, pistachios, cashews and pumpkin seeds.

Fruit Basket: A fruit basket is a classic holiday gift, and a safe bet for business associates, acquaintances and dieters. A basket of wicker, willow or split wood can be filled to overflowing with a variety of fruits and nuts: apples, pears, bananas, a pineapple, dates, pecans and cashews, for instance. You could also include special touches such as a a nutcracker or pretty handmade napkins.

New Neighbor Basket: Here's a great gift idea borrowed from the Welcome Wagon folks. Fill a basket with local maps, tour books and restaurant guides, an address book with emergency numbers (for instructions on how to cover a notebook yourself, see page 44), homemade cookies or quick bread, and deliver it personally to the new neighbor's house. What better way to say "welcome"?

Baby Basket: This makes a special gift for a baby shower or for a new arrival. These baskets can be slanted toward the baby's practical needs with supplies like baby powder, moist towelettes, ointments, a hair brush, a rattle and diaper pins. Or baby baskets can lean more toward the cute, with stuffed animals and clothes such as booties and a bonnet, crib blankets and a rattle.

Get Well Basket: Nobody likes to be sick or convalescing, but a gift basket can help make it slightly more bearable. Send a basket filled with things like cans of chicken soup, bottled orange juice, Vitamin C, aspirin, Alka-Seltzer, an African violet or some other small houseplant, a magazine or puzzle book, note-

Welcome newcomers to your area with this variation on the "New Neighbor Basket." This idea is geared to moving day, before neighbors have had a chance to unpack. Fill a market basket with food staples, fruit and nonperishable items such as soap and aluminum foil. For an extra treat, tuck in some gift certificates to a local fast-food restaurant.

cards and envelopes, a cassette tape or CD, and a big, cheerful Get Well Soon card. (Adapt the contents to the person's condition. The medicinal items like aspirin and Alka-Seltzer should be omitted for people who are seriously ill.)

Bridal Shower Basket: At a wedding, this basket holds all the tiny net packages of birdseed or rice distributed to guests for showering the newlyweds as they make their getaway. But though this gift was designed for a bride, it can be adapted to serve as a bath basket or a letter writer's basket for someone who likes a romantic, Victorian look.

Line a white basket with delicate floral fabric. Glue lace trim around the edge of the basket, and twine satin or grosgrain ribbon around the handle. Tie a multilooped bow at each side of the handle. You might also add satin rosebuds, dried flowers or even little birds. (For additional instructions, see the How-To section.)

Picnic Basket: Fill a split oak picnic basket with goodies such as dried fruits, cookies, chips and snack foods, as well as a festive tablecloth, colorful plastic tableware and glasses. If you want to decorate the basket itself, use a base coat of wood stain or paint. If the gift is for someone with a whimsical bent, consider painting designs on the lid freehand—a grape vine, flowers or a primitive landscape. Another idea is to purchase some small wooden shapes such as ducks or cows at a craft store, then paint them and glue them onto the lid of the basket. You can even paint a background scene on the lid, and use the cutouts as figures in the scene.

Fourth of July Basket: Paint a picnic basket with a Fourth of July theme to give as an all-American gift. Paint stars on the lid and stripes around the sides, and fill it with sparklers, small flags, plastic picnicware, soft drinks, smoked sausage and buns, catsup, mustard and relish.

Bread Basket: This makes a great hostess gift, especially during the holidays. Use a shallow, bowl-like basket; paint or varnish it if you like. Once it dries, open up a napkin and lay it in the bottom of the basket, arranging miniature loaves of different homemade breads (wrapped in clear plastic), muffins, jams, honey and herb butters on top. If you want to go all out, include place mats and a set of the napkins

Anyone with a green thumb will appreciate this gift. Once the seeds have been planted, the flowers fertilized, and the tools put away, the empty basket can be used to transport freshly picked vegetables from the garden to the kitchen.

in the same fabric you used for the liner.

Sports Lover's Basket: Depending on the sport, you could use a fisherman's wicker basket, a bicycle basket, or even a nylon sports bag with a favorite team's insignia on it. Fill the basket with team souvenir items like a sun visor, pens, T-shirt, tie tack, cuff links, key chain or sports paraphernalia like golf tees and balls, gloves, fishing lures, tennis balls and sweatbands. A copy of *Sports Illustrated* or some other sports magazine makes a nice visual touch—a year's subscription would be a monthly reminder of how much you care. You might even tuck in some tickets to the big game!

Beach Basket: Use a big, floppy basket that's easy to carry, and fill it with a beach towel, sunscreen or suntan oil, sunglasses, a paperback novel, and perhaps an inflatable beach ball or float. For a special touch, hot glue seashells onto the front, and line the basket with a colorful fabric before filling.

Letter Writer's Basket: Find a long, shallow basket, then personalize it by pickling, painting, varnishing or spatter painting it, if desired. Depending on the taste of the recipient, you might also add lace, ribbons or dried flowers as decorations. Then, fill the basket with postcards, pens, an address book, sealing wax and seal, stationery, envelopes and commemorative postage stamps as you can see illustrated in the photo on page 13.

Desk Organizer Basket: This basket might be similar in shape to the letter writer's basket, but the contents are more businesslike. This gift includes things like paper clips in a magnetic holder, pens, pencils, notepads, Post-It pads, Liquid Paper, a letter opener and a paperweight. Ideally, the basket should fit in a desk drawer and could be used to keep supplies neat in perpetuity.

Bicyclist's Basket: In one of those old-fashioned bike baskets that fastens onto the handlebars, provide reflector tape, inner tubes, a patch kit, a small handheld pump, bicycle bell, chocolate or "energy" bars, bottled water, Gatorade, handlebar tape, padded bike gloves, socks, a bicyclist's cap and a guide to local bike trails.

Car Lover's Basket: This may not be a basket at all, but a plastic crate that fits in the trunk of the car or on a closet shelf. Fill it with things like Armor All, shop rags, chamois, tar remover, car wax and STP gas

A gourmet basket filled with crackers, condiments and sparkling cider makes a great gift for just about anyone. This one includes potato-printed napkins and placemats for an extra special touch. (For a closer look at these place mats, see the photo on page 79.)

or oil treatment. A chalkboard eraser is great for defogging the insides of windows before the defroster takes effect. Suggest your car lover keep it in the glove box for instant access.

Emergency Basket for Car: For this you'll need a roomy "suitcase style" wicker basket with fasteners, a picnic-style basket, or even a plastic box with a tight fitting lid. Paint, varnish or pickle the basket inside and out, then fill it with a flashlight, flares, jumper cables, road atlas, state and city maps, "Call Police" sign, water bottle and a blanket.

Health Club Basket: A duffel bag or canvas carryall can be used for toting gym clothes back and forth from the club. Fill it with bottled mineral water, sweatbands, a T-shirt or sweatshirt (possibly hand decorated—see Chapter Four for ideas), swimmer's goggles, a workout tape, deodorant, body lotion, luffa and a towel.

Gardener's Basket: In a basket that can transport freshly picked produce or flowers from the garden to the kitchen (page 11), corral things like a trowel, work gloves, garden hat, seed packets of unusual plants such as sunspot dwarf sunflowers, seed starter and cups, bulbs and natural fertilizer.

Flower Basket: Here's a way to dress up a gift of flowers or a houseplant. Use an appropriately shaped basket (tall and narrow) as a container for a potted plant or vase of flowers. You can even make your own log cabin style container (see Chapter Three for more information).

Recycling Basket: This is a politically correct gift for the environmentalists on your list. In a satchel or canvas "basket" (which can be used to transport groceries, thereby saving paper sacks), pack products made from recycled paper and plastic, a water saver attachment for the faucet, some nontoxic, environmentally safe cleansers, and the book *50 Simple Things You Can Do to Save the Earth.*

Pet Basket: This is the perfect gift for an animal lover. In a wicker dog or cat bed, group claw or nail trimmers, brushes, hair ball medicine, dog biscuits, catnip, squeaky toys or plastic balls, and a book about obedience training or animal first aid.

Artist's Basket: In a beautifully woven basket or a tool box, bestow your favorite artist with paintbrushes, paints, a copy of an art magazine, handmade paper, fancy pens, watercolors, charcoal, pencils, an eraser, a sharpener and a sketchpad.

An ideal gift for friends who live far away, a letter writer's basket can include postcards, pens, an address book, stationery, envelopes and commemorative postage stamps.

Music Lover's Basket: In a flat basket (such as a hearth basket) that can be used to store sheet music, include a song book, a small instrument like a harmonica or a hand drum, maracas, tickets to an event, and cassette tapes or CDs.

State Baskets: These are often done by the professionals and feature a variety of products from a particular state. For example, a Wisconsin basket might be packed in a wooden cheese crate and include wild rice, apples, cherry jelly, maple syrup, rye chips and cheeses. A State Basket can be a potpourri of products, or it can be more narrowly defined, with themes like "spices," "sweets," "popcorn," "breakfast," or "pantry supplies." These are all great gifts for friends who've moved away.

Kitchen Basket: This makes a good housewarming or bridal shower gift. Line a basket with dish towels and fill it with utensils—wooden spoons, wire whisks, ladles, spatulas, knife sharpeners and jar openers. Tie a "kitchen witch" doll or a Mexican wheat blessing onto the handle.

Bath Basket: Bath baskets make great gifts for most all women, and even for some men. (You can tell who's a good candidate for this gift by taking a peak at his or her bathroom. If there are lots of toiletries, fancy soaps, bath salts and colognes, the person will appreciate a bath basket.) Fill it with scented soap, bubble bath, body lotion, potpourri, a luffa, back scrubber, nail file, clippers, brush or maybe even cosmetics. To decorate a bath basket, think about the person's favorite colors and home decor, then create something that reflects his or her personal style using paint, fabric, ribbon, dried flowers, whatever!

Valentine's Day Basket: Find a heart-shaped basket, paint it red and embellish it with dried flowers as shown in the photo on page 17. Then, fill the basket with chocolates, candles, bubble bath or aftershave, sexy underwear, maybe even a bottle of champagne, and other goodies to make your sweetie's heart grow fonder.

St. Patrick's Day Basket: To give the luck of the Irish, fill a basket with Irish Creme coffee, a tin of corned beef, Bremner Wafer Crackers, Irish soda bread (for a recipe, see Chapter Five), mints, a shamrock plant, an Irish blessing plaque—anything green. Paint it specially, or just tie on a big green bow.

Graduation Basket: For those about to join "the real world," fill a basket or briefcase with pens, notepads, an address book, a pocket calendar, a calculator, an alarm clock, packets of coffee, and a mug.

Mother's Day Basket: You should tailor the ingredients to suit your mother's taste, but typical contents for this basket can include cologne, hand lotion, hankies, a small photo of you and your family in an attractive frame, a tussie mussie of dried flowers (see Chapter Three), candies, a sachet and a "Best Mother in the World" mug or figurine.

Father's Day Basket: Again, tailor the ingredients in this basket to fit your dad's personality. Some suggestions: aftershave, golf balls, fishing flies, handkerchiefs, tie tack, money clip, joke book, desk accessories, a framed photo and cigars.

Birthday Basket: Many of the baskets described so far would work as birthday presents, but the ingredients should be tailored specifically to the person. Some people like to give gag gifts for milestone years like thirty, forty, fifty, sixty and sixty-five. If that's you, fill a basket with things like Geritol, wrinkle cream, old-timer's hat or mug, etc.

Secretary's Day Basket: Show your secretary how much you appreciate all that hard work by giving a basket filled with a bouquet of fresh or dried flowers, hand lotion, a small sewing kit, a mug, a box of tea, and a jar of candy.

Boss's Day Basket: Say thanks to a super boss with a basket filled with her or his favorite things—such as a book, flowers, golf tees, a pen and pencil set, and notepaper.

Easter Basket: The Easter basket for children is the classic example of the holiday genre: a pastel, striped basket filled with colored eggs, chocolate bunnies, jelly beans, coconut birds' nests, and plush, miniature stuffed animals.

Christmas Basket: This gift provides a nifty solution to the problem of how to display all the Christmas cards. Use a roomy basket that sits flat, tie a big bow out of red, green or plaid ribbon on the handle, and tuck in a sprig of live holly or a silk pine bough with berries. Stand cards up in the front of the basket as they arrive. For an extra special treatment, hot glue pinecones all over the basket.

Halloween Basket: A spooky Halloween basket can be used to hand out candy to trick-or-treaters. Paint it orange and black, or spray it with Carnival

Webbing to look like cobwebs. Then hot glue on lots of creepy critters — rubber rats and snakes, plastic spiders and lizards, glass eyeballs, and other gruesome stuff from the novelty craft store. This basket is guaranteed to give little goblins and ghouls something to squeal about!

BASKET DECORATING HOW-TO'S
Baskets come in all shapes, colors and sizes, and can be further embellished in thousands of ways. Here are some guidelines to help you add your own personal touch and create beautiful gift baskets each and every time.

Using Paint
Use spray paint, or brush on paint or stain, to personalize a store-bought basket. First, sand the basket slightly to help the surface absorb the paint. To spray paint, use light, even, overlapping coats. Don't try to achieve full coverage the first time; several light coats are better than one heavy coat. When using a brush, stroke the paint out thoroughly, poking the bristles in between the weavers. Use paint straight out of the bottle for a "painted," as opposed to dyed, look. Paint the entire basket inside and out. Allow to dry; then repeat if necessary. For a shiny basket, use enamel paint or apply a water-based varnish.

If you're a painter, you may want to add designs to the basket: landscapes or characters on the lids of picnic-style baskets, grapevines or other floral motifs around the edges of flat baskets. Use your imagination and feel free to experiment — remember you can always paint over something if it doesn't live up to your expectations. After painting, be sure to coat your basket with either a brush- or spray-on varnish. Other painting techniques include:

Pickling: For a lighter, more transparent look that lets the wood of your basket show through the paint, try this technique. Dilute paint to transparency (four parts water to one part paint), then brush it on an unfinished basket. Just about any color is suitable for use on light baskets; darker baskets may need a ratio of two parts water to one part paint to be effectively colored. Test your paint on the bottom of the basket first before settling on a mixture.

Another way to achieve a pickled look is to brush on paint straight from the bottle, then while the paint

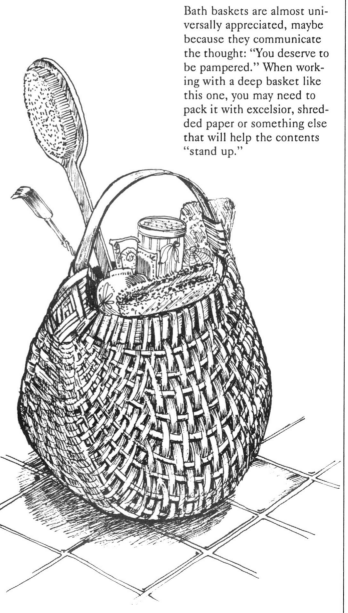

Bath baskets are almost universally appreciated, maybe because they communicate the thought: "You deserve to be pampered." When working with a deep basket like this one, you may need to pack it with excelsior, shredded paper or something else that will help the contents "stand up."

You can use pinecones to decorate all manner of objects. Pictured here: a pinecone frame, basket, candleholder and a potpourri (or paper clip) holder. The plain basket holds firestarter pinecones that were dipped in scented wax. These cones can be kept on the hearth and used as kindling.

Embellishing baskets with paint and dried flowers is easy and
fun to do. This heart-shaped version would be especially appropriate for Valentine's Day or for an engagement, bridal or
shower gift. (See Basket Decorating How-To's, pages 15-22.)

is still wet, rub most of it off with a soft rag. In addition, some companies offer products designed to be used in this way. (Delta offers a variety of shades of transparent pickling gels suitable for use on raw wood or unfinished baskets.) The effect is subtle and elegant.

Antiquing: For a standard "antique" look on a white basket, brush on burnt sienna oil paint thinned with turpentine. As with pickling, rub the basket with a soft cloth to remove most of the paint, leaving it behind in the cracks. To antique or pickle a dark basket, use diluted white paint. Experiment with other light colors on dark baskets, such as yellow, pink and pale blue, diluted at least four to one with turpentine.

Spatter Painting: Use a toothbrush to speckle (spatter paint) a basket. Just base coat the basket in a light color, then choose several coordinated colors to flick onto the surface with a toothbrush. Dip the toothbrush in paint, then rub your thumb back and forth over the bristles to spray droplets of paint onto the basket. You can also use an old pump spray bottle to spatter the paint. Just be sure to cover your work area well, because that paint will fly!

Experimenting: Consider altering a basket's look with commercial spray products. For instance, try webbing with colorful threads that resemble spiderwebs; Fleck-Stone, which produces a granite-like finish; Cracklin' Finish, for the "distressed" look of peeling paint; or Snow-tex, which looks like snow. Browse around a craft store and see what's available. You're sure to come up with some unique products to try on your baskets.

Using Fabric

You can use fabric in a variety of ways to enhance a gift basket. Line the inside of a basket with calico, decorate the outside with a design motif cut from cloth, wrap the handle with satin ribbon, or glue on a big lace bow. These ideas will work on painted or shellacked baskets, as well as on raw, unpainted ones. However, if you plan to paint the basket, do so before adding fabric.

Choose cloth with a color and pattern that suits the recipient's taste as well as the basket idea you have planned. Take along a fabric scrap when shopping for the contents of the basket so you can color coordinate these items. Fabric helps create a pulled together, designer look that always gets rave reviews. Here are a few suggestions:

Design Motifs: Fusible web is an iron-on product that prevents fabric from raveling or fraying. This makes it easy for you to cut a fabric motif out, then use it to decorate baskets (and clothing) without laborious hemming. Sold at fabric stores, fusible web comes with instructions.

First, look for fabric with a distinct pattern that will be easy to cut out. Inexpensive bandanas or scraps of cloth left over from sewing projects are good candidates. Following the manufacturer's directions, iron the fusible web onto the fabric. Cut out the patterns you plan to use; then pull the fabric away from the fusible web backing.

Next, use white glue to attach the fabric patterns to the basket. Then, you can use dimensional fabric paints in matching or coordinating colors to highlight or accent the patterns. Paint the fabric on only one side of the basket at a time; allow it to dry flat for four to six hours before painting the other side. For an example, see the basket on page 47.

To line the basket, you can cut out fabric shapes as you did for the outside, and glue them in place. Or you can use a bandana or scarf intact, as a removable liner; similarly, hem a large fabric scrap—or fray the edges artfully—and toss that in the bottom of the basket, with the edges peeking out. A few more options follow.

Basket Lining: If you're going to paint the basket, or decorate it in some other way, do that first. Then line the basket with fabric to highlight the contents. Sometimes you can simply lay the fabric in place, then hot glue or hand stitch it into place, forming darts or tucks in the corners. The top edge can be turned over or finished with lace. Or you can allow lots of extra material and gather it to form a kind of ruffle that sticks up over the top of the basket.

For a more fitted lining, measure your basket, then cut fabric pieces for the sides and bottom, adding an inch for seam allowances. Baste the pieces together and check for fit; make any necessary adjustments, then sew up the fabric. To attach the lining fabric, use large stitches to loosely sew it in place. (For yet another lining method, see Fabric Stiffener.)

Fabric Stiffener: This product is often used to make bows and other fabric decorations droop-free forever. Fabric stiffener is a liquid that, once applied to fabric and allowed to dry, makes the fabric stay in whatever shape you create.

When lining a basket using fabric stiffener, cover your work surface with plastic to protect it from drips. Position the fabric inside the basket, then brush on a fabric stiffener such as Stiffy or Drape N' Shape. Apply the product liberally, until the fabric is saturated. If necessary, hold the fabric in place with clothespins or clamps. Once it dries, brush on water-based varnish for a matte sheen or a glossy look, if you want.

To make bows that will stay perky for years, follow the above instructions, but don't place the bow on the basket until the bow is dry; at that point, hot glue it in place.

Skirts: Some baskets look sweet wearing skirts — with material on the outside instead of the inside. To make a skirt, measure the top rim of your basket and cut a length of material twice as long. Hem the bottom and gather the top (machine baste or use a large running stitch and pull the thread to gather), then hot glue the top of the skirt onto the basket. Add accents of ribbon or lace. You can finish the handle by wrapping it with ribbon or lace. Another option is to hem both sides of a long, narrow strip of fabric. (It should be twice as long as the handle.) Next, sew a loose running stitch up the center of the strip and pull it tight to gather; attach this ruffle to the handle with hot glue.

Ribbons and Bows: Wrap ribbon around the handle and rim of a basket for an old-fashioned, romantic look. Twist several colors of ribbon together for added visual excitement. Hot glue the ends and several other inconspicuous spots to hold the ribbons in place; add bows or silk or dried flowers for an extra special touch.

Using a Hot Glue Gun

Mini glue guns can be had for less than ten dollars at craft and hobby stores, and they are worth their weight in gold. The adhesive is much stronger than white or other craft glues, so it's easy to attach flowers, seeds, pinecones, fabric and other, heavier stuff you'd never have dreamed possible before. But be careful — that glue is hot! If your glue gun didn't come with a stand, use a glass plate, mug, or other nonflam-mable surface to rest it on when you aren't using it.

While the gun is heating up, cover your work surface with newspaper. Then use gentle pressure on the trigger to release the adhesive. Hold larger items in place for a minute to be sure of the bond; heavier stuff should probably be wired in place with florist wire, then glued for reinforcement. Don't worry about those little strands of glue that trail all over the place as you're working; they'll come off easily later, after they harden.

Pinecones, Cinnamon Sticks and Other Found Objects: Found objects can be as clever and as zany as you please, including everything from pebbles, shells and pasta shapes to novelty items like gumball trinkets and rubber spiders. Pinecones are great because they can either be purchased or you can gather them yourself; cinnamon sticks smell good and are fairly inexpensive.

The general rule for gluing on objects is to work on one side of the basket at a time, keeping that side level as the glue dries. (Use a bowl or a stack of books to prop the basket securely on its side.) If you're using objects of varying sizes, begin with larger items, then fill in the gaps with medium and smaller ones.

Keep gluing until that side is completely covered, then move to the next side. Continue adding objects until the basket is covered. To finish the basket, glue small and medium objects around the rim, being careful to maintain a balanced look. Follow a similar procedure up the sides of the handle, leaving the bottom side of the handle bare, near the top, where the hand grasps it.

Silk and Dried Flowers: Decorating a basket with flowers is a beautiful way to dress it up. Silk flowers can easily be wired around the rim or handle of the basket. They come in a rainbow of colors that can be coordinated with any scheme, and work well in combination with ribbons.

When working with dried flowers, begin by gluing little pieces of sphagnum or Spanish moss all around the rim of the basket. This will form a base to glue the flowers into. Poke the ends of the flowers into the moss; secure with a dollop of glue. Look for curves in the stems of the flowers that echo the shape of the basket, and arrange them accordingly. Alternate the direction that you stick the flowers into the moss for a lush, dimensional look. Trim stems that stick out.

Flowers can be pressed, dried and even made into paper! Consider a framed collection of pressed flowers—like this one by Ann McSwiggin—a gift that brings the outdoors inside all year round. Or used dried flowers to make your own paper. The homemade paper in the basket gets its color and texture from potpourri, which was added to the pulp.

I used an old five-pound coffee can and sticks I gathered myself to make this twig planter. Filled with dried flowers, it makes a unique gift and a wonderful home accessory. (Complete instructions are on page 39.)

Once the basket is pretty well covered, glue on your "accent" flowers—your favorites, or the most dramatic ones, or those you have the fewest of. Work in a star pattern all over the rim rather than in a straight line around the basket. That way, if you miscalculate and run out of accent flowers, the piece will still look good because it was developed as you went along. (For more gift ideas using dried flowers, see Chapter Three.)

BASKET BASICS

Here are some general tips to help make gift baskets easier and more fun to make.

•To find the best basket for your purposes, match a type of basket (shape, color, size, material) to your specific idea. Think about what kinds of things the basket will hold, and look for one that will show off these objects. Smaller baskets are often better because they quickly look full—even when they only contain a couple of items. And don't be above recycling old baskets you may have around the house. By the time you finish decorating it and filling it with gifts, your old basket will have a new incarnation, and its old personality will be totally obscured.

•Sometimes you can use a book, a piece of jewelry, or some other "main attraction" gift to clearly state the theme of a basket.

•Think about your color scheme when making or purchasing goodies to fill the basket. Take along a swatch of fabric or a paint chip to help keep you on track. By staying within a certain palette of colors, your gift basket will have a pulled together "designer" look.

•Organize your shopping trip to get the most for both your time and money. Make a list of all the items you hope to include; add a couple of alternate ideas in case you can't find everything you want. Shop discount drug and department stores for gift items; be alert for sales and specials. For instance, save those free gifts of cosmetics from department stores (given when you purchase a certain amount of merchandise) to use in future bath baskets.

•Before packing the basket with gifts, you may want to fill it with tissue paper, shredded paper, Easter grass, or packing grass to make sure individual items sit up high enough to be seen. Another idea is to wrap the basket in clear plastic "oyster" paper and tie it up with a bow. If the gift is to be a surprise, wrap the basket in several layers of tissue paper, or put it in a big box and wrap that. Another option is to wrap items individually before placing them in the basket.

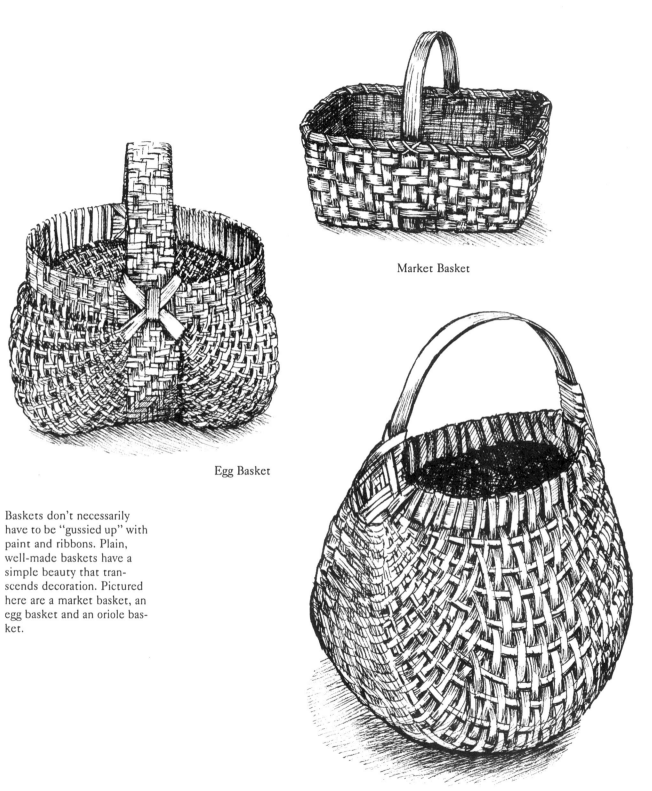

Market Basket

Egg Basket

Baskets don't necessarily have to be "gussied up" with paint and ribbons. Plain, well-made baskets have a simple beauty that transcends decoration. Pictured here are a market basket, an egg basket and an oriole basket.

Oriole Basket

Gifts from the garden make good scents. Debbie Vitkow
Davidson created this wreath using a wire wreath form, dried
apples, eucalyptus, statice, cinnamon sticks, whole nutmegs
and a raffia bow; you'll find instructions for making your own
on pages 35-37. Pomanders such as those in the basket are
easy and quick to make — all you need are oranges or apples
and whole cloves.

A pepper wreath makes a nice gift for your favorite chef. I got this idea from a catalog, where the dried pepper wreath had a price tag of forty-five dollars. I bought a straw wreath form and twelve dollars worth of dried peppers at the supermarket. Then I used a hot glue gun to attach the peppers. As you can see, I overlapped the peppers around the circle so they faced the same direction. (When objects have the same distinct shape—such as bay leaves or peppers, for instance—it's important to work in one direction only.) When you're finished, spray the wreath with an acrylic glaze.

THREE

GIFTS FROM THE GARDEN

*G*ardeners know the peaceful, contented feeling you get in the presence of living plants. Though subtle, it can't be denied. For them, giving presents of plants or homegrown produce is a natural metaphor for a gift of life and love. But even if your thumb is purple, you can use both dried and live plants and flowers to make wonderfully personal gifts.

In this chapter, you'll find gift ideas that range from living plants to primitive home accessories. Many of the gifts involve crafty uses for dried plants. You'll find a variety of wreaths, topiaries, centerpieces and accessories—everything from cinnamon stick desk accessories to pressed flower pendants and dried flower hair barrettes. If you buy plant materials already dried, the basics can be pretty pricey, depending on how big a piece you're making. However, if you grow the plants yourself, or gather them from the wild, the cost goes down to next to nothing. (For food gift ideas from the garden, see Chapter Five.)

One word of warning: A few people have allergies that interfere with their enjoyment of plants, both live and dried. Because plants collect dust, people with housedust allergies are advised not to keep any kind of plant—not even silk flowers. And someone who's allergic to straw would not appreciate a wreath made on a straw base. Some plants, like goldenrod, can set off sneezing fits in an allergy sufferer when they are used in indoor arrangements. Try to ascertain whether someone fits any of these categories by looking around his or her home to see if there are any plants or dried flowers, or, if there's any doubt, casually inquire of the person herself. It's always better to be safe than sorry.

Gifts of live and dried plants are especially appropriate on Valentine's Day and for birthdays, but they're suitable for any occasion. The following list provides some possibilities, but remember to generate your own ideas before settling on "the perfect gift."

IDEAS

Cactus Garden: This is a great gift for earthy people who forget to water their houseplants. In a ceramic pot or bowl (possibly hand decorated), plant barrel cactus, zebra plants and cereus. Add a pretty rock and a small sprig of dried flowers for color—something like red celosia looks good. (Note: to transplant a cactus, wrap a towel around it several times, then make a "noose" out of the towel and lift the plant up gently. Use a spoon to press dirt down around the roots.)

Windowsill Herb Garden: Here's a fun and useful idea for your favorite cook. Just plant small flowerpots with basil, thyme, dill and chives and give a miniature herb garden that will sit on a sunny windowsill and provide fresh herbs year round. If you start far enough in advance, you can plant seeds. You may want to plant several windowsill gardens at the same time so you'll have this gift on hand. Otherwise, purchase small plants and transplant them into clay pots.

Wintertime Bouquet: Plant bulbs such as hyacinth, crocus, daffodil, tulip, amaryllis or narcissus in a container in the autumn for brilliant winter blooms. (See the How-To section later in this chapter for more information.)

Wreaths: Wreaths aren't just for holidays anymore. They're used outdoors and in, on doors, walls, windows and even on the table as a centerpiece. You can make wreaths out of just about anything, so they can be tailored specifically to the recipient's taste. For example, for someone who loves to cook, make a gourmet wreath of dried herbs including basil, dill, parsley, tarragon, oregano, thyme and garlic—or what about a wreath made entirely of bay leaves tied with red ribbon? You can make wreaths out of eucalyptus and baby's breath, grapevines and bittersweet, or bunny tail grass and roses. And speaking of roses, if you're a gardener, consider making a wreath entirely of roses—simply dip full blooms in silica gel.

When you consider all the wreath-making possibilities—evergreens, flowers, herbs, vines, twigs, cones, pods and adding ribbon, bows and novelties—it can seem a little overwhelming. But follow your instincts, and don't be afraid to try unconventional ideas. Here are a few wreath combinations to get you thinking:

- Evergreen with dried roses
- Pussy willows with dried roses
- Heart wreath of dried roses, or one with a mix of flowers
- Wheat wreath, or a miniature sheaf that is tied for hanging
- Magnolia leaves and silk flowers
- Baby shower wreath of baby's breath or statice

- Pinecone wreath
- Dried apple wreath
- Centerpiece of evergreen, acorns, walnuts and pinecones
- Seeded wreath for the birds
- Seashells and eucalyptus
- Gourds, sunflowers and bittersweet
- Hard candy and lollipops with ribbon curls
- Living wreath planted with succulents and ivy
- A rosemary plant that has been trained to grow in a circular shape
- Fabric scrap wreath (see Chapter Four)

Remember that many of these ideas can be adapted into swags, hearth blessings, topiaries, etc. To find specific instructions on how to make wreaths and their other forms, see the How-To section on pages 33-38.

Dried Flower Arrangements: As an everlasting reminder of friendship, give a dried flower arrangement. Simple pots and baskets filled with lavender, wheat, larkspur or sweet Annie make great decorations for tables and mantels. Or combine different plants and flowers for a breathtaking centerpiece. As

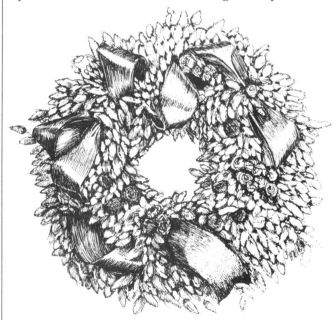

Wreaths can be made from just about anything. Consider this one, which was crafted of bunny tail grass and dried roses, then accented with a wide, metallic ribbon.

with wreaths, the range of materials you can use is mind-boggling, especially considering the variety of possible containers. Some arrangements are actually inspired by vases—which can be everything from antique ewers, painted bowls and ceramic crockery to twig planters, jam jars and even hollowed-out pumpkins. (The pumpkin would serve only as the outer "shell," with the arrangement secured in a can or bowl inside.)

Use floral foam to support the arrangement. Thick-stemmed flowers can be stuck directly in the foam, while more delicate plant stems will need to be reinforced with wire or floral picks first. (See the How-To section later in this chapter.)

Bouquets and Tussie Mussies: Full-size bouquets of dried flowers make dramatic gifts on birthdays, Mother's Day and other festive occasions. Similar to wreaths and arrangements in their versatility, sometimes the same plants will look completely different in combination with other plants. Door bouquets include ribbons for tying them onto doors, a bedpost or the wall.

Tussie mussies are miniature bouquets used in gift baskets, to top packages (see page 98), with a get well card, or all by themselves as a token of affection. A tussie mussie has at least three miniature bouquets bound or wired together as one. Ultrafeminine, they look nice on vanities and in bathrooms. (For instructions, see page 37.)

Topiaries: Topiaries are perfect in Victorian and traditional decors, and they make great gifts for anyone with a romantic streak. Like wreaths, they offer limitless possibilities. You can interpret them seasonally, with different materials in different sizes. Let your imagination be your guide in creating unique topiary decorations such as the one pictured on page 91. (See pages 37-38 for specific instructions.)

Baskets: Baskets look beautiful when embellished with dried flowers, and a glue gun makes it so easy! Refer to Chapter Two, pages 19-22, for specific how-to advice.

Hair Ornaments: These romantic accessories are perfect for brides, and for romantic little girls. Hot glue small pieces of delicate flowers like statice, clover blossoms, rosemary, miniature roses and caspia onto a plastic headband or hair comb. (For an example, see page 46.)

Straw Hats With Flowers: Often hung on front doors in summertime in place of a wreath, and sometimes worn by bride's maids (and on Kentucky Derby Day), old-fashioned straw hats look sweet boasting small bouquets or encircled with flowers. Use hot glue or wire to attach the flowers, and add trailing ribbons to complete the look.

Pomanders: These add a wonderful spicy scent to kitchens or closets. Apples can be stuck with cinnamon, oranges with cloves; lemons and quinces can also be used. Pierce the thick skins of citrus fruits with a fork, a nail or a small knitting needle before studding the fruit with whole spice. When the fruit is completely covered with cloves or cinnamon sticks, roll it in ground spices. Tie the pomander with ribbon and secure the ribbon with hot glue; now it's ready to hang or it can be placed in a basket (see the photo on page 24).

Potpourri: Although potpourri is widely available commercially, it's fun to create your own blends. You can make floral fragrance blends, woodsy and exotic scents, even moth-repellant mixtures. Several recipes are included in the How-To section, and potpourri itself can be used in a variety of ways—read on!

Potpourri Ornament: These unique ornaments make great Christmas gifts for friends and coworkers. Use one of the recipes for potpourri on page 37-38 or buy a ready-made mix. You'll just need to remove the top of a clear glass ornament (available at craft stores), then carefully push potpourri into the bulb. Next, glue on a ribbon, small pinecones or silk flowers, then a ribbon for hanging. For extra security, glue the little metal top onto the ornament itself.

Sachets: These fragrant little "pillows" are wonderful scenters for drawers and closets. Just make a little pillow shape from a piece of cloth, sew up three sides, stuff with potpourri, and stitch up the final side. You can make sachets from pretty scraps you have on hand, or from old hankies, doilies, net, ribbon and lace. They can be embroidered, crocheted, knitted, batiked, printed, appliquéd or even photo-transferred. (See Chapter Four for more fabric decoration ideas.)

You can also make "ribbon sachets" by placing two wide (at least 2 inches across) cloth ribbons on top of each other, right sides facing, and sewing up

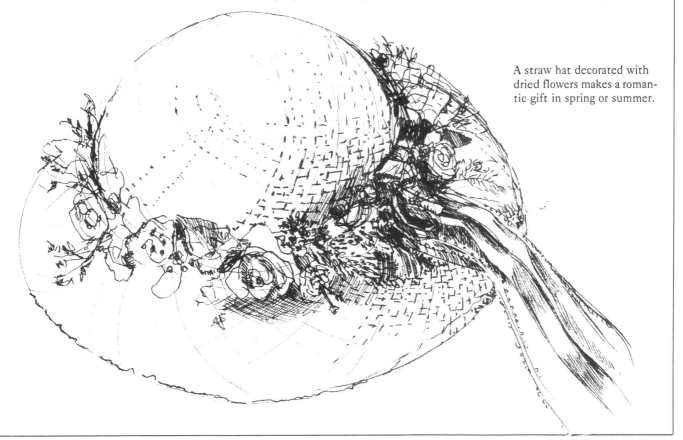

A straw hat decorated with dried flowers makes a romantic gift in spring or summer.

both sides and one end to form a tube. Turn the tube inside out by pushing a dowel or pencil through it to reveal the right sides of the ribbon, then stuff the tube with scented powder that you make by adding a few drops of essential oil to some cornstarch. Mix the powder and oil well, before spooning the mixture into the ribbon tube. Be sure to use essential oil, which is available at craft stores where potpourri is sold and at scent shops such as Crabtree and Evelyn or Caswell Massey. Do not use cologne or perfume because they contain alcohol and will evaporate.

Yet another way to make a sachet is to wrap a scented candle in pretty fabric, then tie the ends with lace or ribbon. If the fragrance of the candle isn't potent enough, boost it with a few drops of essential oil before wrapping it with fabric.

Sweet Sleep Pillows: Make a sachet the size of a pillow and stuff it with mildly scented herbs—chamomile, mugwort, rose geranium leaves, anything subtle. These scented pillows can help cure headaches and promote sweet dreams. It's a good idea to put the herb in an inner pouch of muslin, then to make the pillow out of another fabric. A zipper provides ease in laundering.

Muslin Bath Bags: Stitch up some little muslin bags, or buy some at a health food store (sold as natural, reusable tea bags). Stuff them with chamomile (which is good for the skin), rosemary or mint (which relaxes and invigorates), rose petals or some other flower or herb. When placed under hot tap water in the bathtub, the bags will release a wonderful fragrance. You can also give a jar of the herb to use for refills.

Potpourri Padded Hangers: Make sweet-smelling hangers for women, and piney, cedar scented hangers for men. Simply sew up tubes of decorative fabric, thread them onto hangers, then stuff with potpourri. This is a great gift for romantics and clothes-horses. (For more specific instructions, see Chapter Four.)

Mirrors: Surround a mirror with dried flowers for a romantic gift that looks great in bathrooms, frilly bedrooms and Victorian decors. Simply cover the frame with wire mesh and wire small bunches of flowers into place. Or attach Spanish or sphagnum moss to the edge of the mirror, then hot glue flowers into place. (See Chapter Two for specific how-to instruc-tions on hot gluing.) Use a fixative such as Krylon, available at craft and art supply stores, for dried flowers that will be used outdoors or in a moist location, like the bathroom.

Candlesticks: Use dried flowers to decorate candlesticks seasonally or just for some added romance. Wire garlands of flowers onto simple candlesticks, or create a candle ring centerpiece incorporating candlesticks with a wreathlike arrangement that sits flat. Look at flea markets and secondhand stores for those old-fashioned spools of thread that have large, flat ends with perfect candle-sized holes in them. These make good bases for dried flower decorations.

More Dried Flower Projects: You can use dried flowers to decorate an endless array of objects—stoneware crocks, antique school bells, bookends, old watering cans, you name it! Simply hot glue dried flowers onto the handle, around the rim, or into the opening, as suggested by the specific object; also add ribbons or lace if appropriate. You may be able to combine an object that relates to someone's interest, wooden spoons for a cook, for instance, with a beautiful arrangement of dried flowers. Give your imagination free rein and see what happens.

Pressed Flower Pictures: Give a gift of eternal summer with a beautiful arrangement of pressed flowers. Pressed flowers are used in a variety of craft projects: framed arrangements or collages, greeting cards and gift tags, paper weights, boxes, bookmarks, on serving trays, place mats, napkin rings and coasters—even on flowerpots, furniture, home accessories, jewelry and shoes. Many of these specialty items are sold in craft stores, but others (boxes and flowerpots, for instance), can be found anywhere. Gifts of pressed flowers make great gifts for weddings and birthdays. For tips on pressing flowers, see pages 33-34.

Napkin Rings: Hot glue ribbon and miniature arrangements of dried flowers onto a set of napkin rings to create beautiful table accessories. Remember that you don't have to use all the same kinds of flowers on every napkin ring, but can feature miniature roses on one and rosemary sprigs on another, for instance. You can unify all the designs by using the same accent flowers, something like artemisia or baby's breath. These are great gifts for bridal showers, because the bride may use them at her table at the reception.

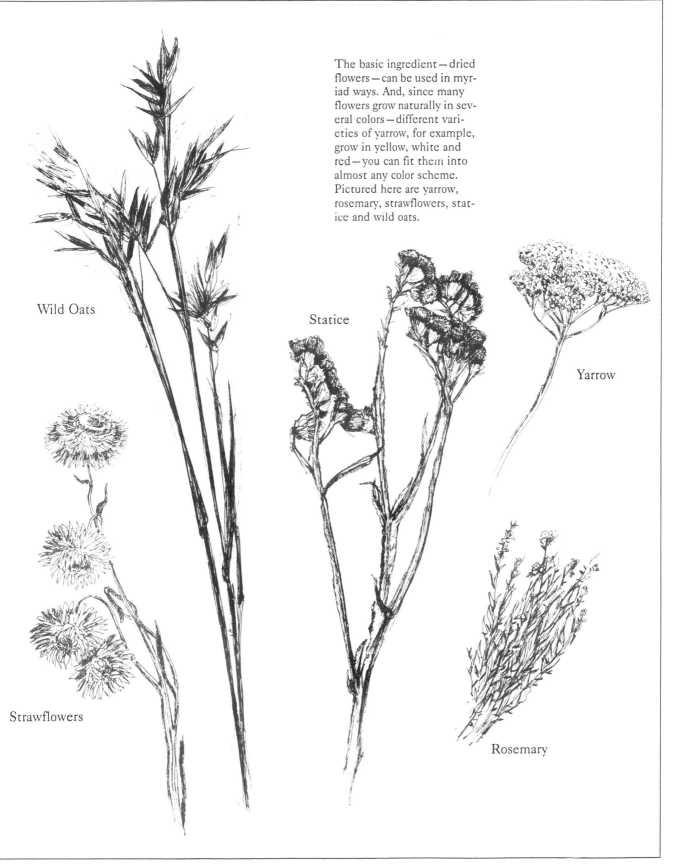

The basic ingredient—dried flowers—can be used in myriad ways. And, since many flowers grow naturally in several colors—different varieties of yarrow, for example, grow in yellow, white and red—you can fit them into almost any color scheme. Pictured here are yarrow, rosemary, strawflowers, statice and wild oats.

Wild Oats

Statice

Yarrow

Strawflowers

Rosemary

You can also use pressed flowers to make unique table accessories. Look for clear Lucite napkin rings at a craft store, the kind with an opening that allows a piece of paper to slip inside. (Similar to those small, freestanding picture frames made of Lucite.) Mount flower arrangements—or even just one flower, surrounded by a decorative border—on paper cut to fit the napkin rings. Cover the paper with clear, heavy-duty, protective tape, such as that used for wrapping packages, and insert paper in the Lucite mounts. An alternate method is to glue pressed flowers onto a wooden or plastic napkin ring, then shellac it several times for protection.

Paperweights: These make nice, small gifts, and add a personal touch to a desk organizer or letter writer's basket, as discussed in Chapter Two. Pressed flower paperweights are easy to make. Just purchase a hollow glass mold at a craft store and trace its outline onto a piece of mat board. Cut this out and arrange your pressed flowers on it, then glue them in place. Use craft cement or hot glue to affix the glass mold. Once this dries, glue a circle of felt on the bottom.

Greeting Cards: Make unique greeting cards and gift tags with pressed flowers and plants. Simply press the flowers as described on pages 33-34, then glue them onto heavy stock paper that's been folded into a card shape. Use blank greeting cards, available at art supply stores, or make your own out of heavy paper. If desired, finish the cards with a water-based varnish to keep them intact and "shiny" looking.

Door Plates: Use pressed flowers to decorate the plates that protect swinging doors from finger marks. Available from craft suppliers, these specially designed Lucite plates can be decorated to suit any room. Cut a piece of foam to fit the center of the plate, without overlapping the holes in the corners (for the screws that fasten the plate to the door). The foam will help press the flowers tight against the plastic surface. Use heavy paper or card stock in a decorative color that complements your flowers and cut it to fit the plate. Punch holes in the corners of the paper to match the holes on the door plate. Glue pressed flowers onto the card stock, and assemble.

More Pressed Flower Projects: Just about anything flat can be decorated with pressed flowers—pendants, earrings, candlesticks, lamp shades, chair backs, even high heels. Look for special backings and templates at the craft store, or simply glue flowers onto objects like chairs, then protect them with several coats of varnish.

Pressed Autumn Leaves: The beautiful flaming colors of fall can be preserved in a variety of gifts. Use autumn leaves to cover boxes, cans, even trunks, or adapt the projects already listed for pressed flowers—door plates, greeting cards, pictures, etc. For instructions, see the How-To section of this chapter.

Natural Twig Pot Wraps: As you can see in the photo on page 21, vine-wrapped vases and twig-covered pots make beautiful containers to dress up plant gifts and dried arrangements. Simply use hot glue to attach sticks onto an old coffee can. For detailed instructions, see the How-To section.

Rustic Home Accessories: You can make a beautiful centerpiece, plant stand or end table out of sticks you've gathered. All use the same log cabin construction technique of stacking sticks; the only difference is in size and scale. See the How-To section for more information. (The planter is illustrated on pages 7 and 38.)

Fire Starter Pinecones: A great gift for anyone with a fireplace, these pinecones look good in a basket. Gather or purchase pinecones; make sure they're dry before beginning. Melt paraffin in the top of a double boiler, adding a red crayon for color and a few drops of cinnamon essential oil for scent. Once the paraffin has completely melted, grasp a pinecone firmly using some old tongs or a coat hanger that's been bent to form a handle. Dip the pinecone into the wax, then allow it to dry on a sheet of waxed paper. Repeat the process to create a set of cones.

Walnut Shell Rattle: This makes a great gift for musicians, especially percussionists, as well as for anyone with a taste for the unusual. Start with whole English walnuts, in the shell. Use a nutcracker to open the shells or use a sharp knife to cut them in half. Remove the nut meat, and put aside. (See Chapter Five for recipes using walnuts.) Drill a hole in the center of each walnut half, then thread jute, yarn or heavy string through each hole, knotting the end. Hold all the separate strings so that the ends are even, then twist this bundle and knot it back on itself to form a handle. (If you know macrame, you can create a fancy knotted handle, but this isn't required.)

Gourd Crafts: Colorful, fancifully shaped gourds

appear fresh in supermarkets every fall. They make wonderful festive centerpieces that usually last for several months before the gourds begin to mold. Most people pitch their centerpiece at that point, but if they'd be patient and wipe the mold off regularly with a paper towel, they would soon have dried gourds that can be used in a variety of craft projects.

Cut a large gourd in half to make a bowl to hold potpourri, for instance. Or create a permanent centerpiece by painting a variety of gourds to mimic their original coloring. Or make a rattle, painted either with designs or with the gourd's original color. When making a rattle with a stick handle, be sure to remove all the fibers on the inside of the gourd, and add navy beans as well as the seeds if you want a sharp percussive sound. Attach the stick with a glue gun or with melted beeswax.

HOW-TO'S

As you've seen, there are a variety of ways to use plants—both living and dried—to make unique gifts. This section will give all the specifics you'll need to create beautiful gifts from the garden.

Pressing Fresh Flowers

Pressing flowers is easy and fun to do. The main thing you need is patience, because the process takes about six weeks. Almost all plants and flowers, with the exception of succulents, can be pressed, though some blossoms will fade or change color. Yellow flowers, such as buttercups and daffodils, and pink flowers, such as red clover and morning glories, usually retain color well. (Red flowers tend to turn brown, blue flowers often turn pale pink or beige.) Pansies, black-eyed Susans, cosmos, daisies, heather, lavender, Queen Anne's lace and zinnias all press well. Experiment by pressing a variety of flowers and foliage, and see what works best.

Begin by gathering flowers from your garden or the wild, or purchase them from the florist. If you're picking flowers yourself, it's best to gather them at midday, after the dew has evaporated. (Flowers must be dry to press well.) Make sure they're in full bloom and haven't begun to fade. Some large flowers, such as daffodils, will need to be cut up in order to lay flat—you'll put them back together when you make your arrangement. Also, always cut apart stems and

You can make your own flower press out of plywood and eight-inch bolts with washers and wing nuts. Drill holes in the corners of two pieces of wood. Thread the bolts through the holes in one piece of wood, securing the bolts with small dots of glue near their heads. Sandwich your flowers between layers of blotting paper, newspaper and cardboard, place the layers within the press, then fasten on the top and place the wing nuts on the screws and tighten them. Put the press in an out-of-the-way area for six weeks; then you'll have beautiful pressed flowers to use in a variety of projects.

leaves and press them separately from the blossoms; reassemble them later. Roses, by the way, should be pulled apart and pressed as petals.

Here are three ways to press flowers:

Method 1: Arrange flowers of equal thickness on a sheet of blotting paper so they aren't touching each other. (I use bond paper with at least a 25 percent rag content.) Put another piece of paper on top, then carefully place them between the pages of a large book. Make name tags listing the types of flowers and greenery for each layer. For instance, "Rose petals — pink" and "Buttercup — stems." Use these tags like bookmarks for easy retrieval of specific dried materials. Pile bricks and weights on top of the book and leave it alone for six weeks.

Method 2: If you have more flowers than can comfortably fit inside a book's binding, you can improvise a flower press using books, bricks and weights. Just arrange flowers between two sheets of blotting paper, then add a layer of newspaper on either side. Repeat this layering process until all your flowers have been arranged. Place all the newspaper and blotting paper "sandwiches" on a firm surface, with a layer of newspaper beneath the first group of flowers. Then pile heavy books on top of the stack, adding bricks, or concrete blocks if you don't have enough books. Make a little sign: "Flowers pressing — do not disturb" and mark it with the date. Make tags for each layer, as described for Method 1.

Method 3: Perhaps the best way to press flowers is to use a flower press, which you can make yourself or purchase from a craft store for about ten dollars. To make one yourself, simply cut two pieces of plywood, 12 inches square. Clamp the pieces together and drill holes in the corners as shown in the illustration on page 33. Separate the two pieces of wood, then thread 8-inch bolts into the holes of the bottom one. To secure the bolts, add a dab of glue to the bottom threads just before screwing them into place. Cut rectangles of newspaper, blotting paper, and corrugated cardboard to fit within the area between the screws, then make "sandwiches" of flowers to be pressed as described in Method 2. (Use the corrugated cardboard to separate layers of newspapers.) Write tags to identify the different flowers. Then secure the top board with washers and wing nuts. Screw the top on tightly and put the press aside for at least

six weeks or more.

When your flowers are done, disassemble the "sandwiches" carefully, separating the blotting paper and the newspaper. Use a cake spatula or the blunt end of a knife to pick up the pressed flowers, then handle them with tweezers. Now, sort your flowers by color and type, and begin planning your design. Sometimes your gift idea will dictate the size and shape of your design — things like paperweights and pendants provide limited space for interpretation. But place mats, pictures to be framed, and other, larger projects can be done in a number of different ways. So try several arrangements, such as a circular design, an overall pattern, or one that's long and narrow, before making a final decision.

If you're using background material of cloth or paper, choose a color that complements the flowers. Do so even if you're planning a solid design, since little glimmers of it may show through. Trace the inside opening of the frame or the paperweight, pendant or other object you intend to use onto the paper or card stock, then cut the paper to fit the object. This will be your image area.

Arrange all the flowers to your satisfaction before you begin gluing them down. Place smaller background pieces first, then finish with foreground flowers. Next, glue everything carefully in place, and allow to dry.

Paint or otherwise finish your frame, or assemble your paperweight, place mats, etc. Some printers will laminate dried flowers into bookmarks, coasters or even place mat shapes for you. Check under "Printers" in the Yellow Pages and call to discuss your ideas first.

Store pressed flowers in the clear glassine bags used by photographers to store negatives.

Drying Fresh Flowers
To dry fresh herbs and flowers, pick them before they're fully mature. The simplest drying technique is to hang them upside down in a dry, well-ventilated room for several weeks. Or, you can use silica gel, a sandlike substance sold in craft stores that draws moisture out of flowers. (Sterilized children's play sand is a suitable substitute.) Place an inch of silica gel or play sand in a pan, place the flowers on top,

then carefully cover the flowers with more silica gel. Put the pan in a warm place for several weeks until all the moisture is removed. (The silica gel prevents the flowers' petals from withering, but colors may fade slightly.) The drying process can be speeded up somewhat by placing the pan with flowers and silica gel in a 200 degree oven for several hours. Some people even use the microwave.

To prevent flowers that were dried in silica gel or sand from reabsorbing moisture, spray them with a matte fixative such as Krylon, available at craft and art supply stores. Also use fixative on dried flowers that will be used outdoors or in a moist location, such as the bathroom.

Preserving Evergreens

To make sure plants such as pine, holly, ivy and magnolia maintain their bright green color, preserve them with glycerine. (Glycerine is a syrupy liquid and a common skin softening ingredient of cosmetics. It's sold in large drug stores.) Fill a jar with three parts water to one part glycerine. Make an angular cut in the plant stem, and stick the stem in the jar. Leave the branch in place for about two weeks, checking to see if you need to add more water. The colors may darken slightly, but your greens will be preserved. Short stems can be hot glued onto projects. Heavier pieces may need to be wired.

Using Floral Picks and Wire

Floral picks are used to attach delicate dried flowers to a wreath form. You simply wire the plant material to the pick, then stick the pick into the straw, Styrofoam or vine wreath base. Sometimes a dot of hot glue helps reinforce the connection.

Use floral wire to stabilize weak stemmed flowers and those to be dried in sand or silica gel. Cut the stem down to an inch or two, and use a small piece of florist wire to bind another length of florist wire onto the stem. Cover the juncture with florist's tape, if desired. You can stick the wire directly into the hollow stems of flowers like amaranthus.

Floral wire is also used to attach heavy items to wreath frames. Thin or medium gauges work best. Try to find an inconspicuous place to wrap the wire around the item, then twist the excess wire around the wreath base to attach it.

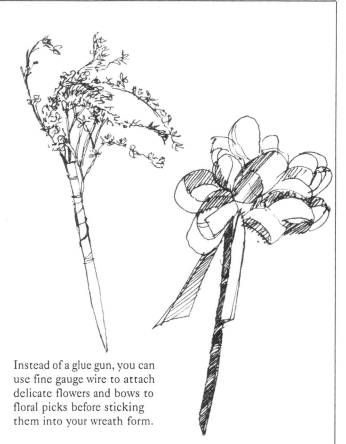

Instead of a glue gun, you can use fine gauge wire to attach delicate flowers and bows to floral picks before sticking them into your wreath form.

Making a Wreath

You can make wreaths from anything your heart desires—dried herbs, flowers, vines, pinecones or teasel, to name just a few. Use or adapt one of the formulas that follow, or make up your own, using whatever herbs and flowers are available in your own garden. A hot glue gun makes it easy to be creative, since most wreath materials can be quickly and simply glued into place. (Note: When making edible wreaths, such as the Kitchen wreath described on page 36, use florist picks to attach the dried plants, never a glue gun.)

Start with a straw, wire or Styrofoam wreath form; you can also make an exotic looking base from kudzu or grapevine. Make a hanger by twisting florist wire around the wreath form, creating a loop. Next, use a glue gun to attach small clusters of flowers or herbs, or wire them onto florist's picks and push them into the inner and outer edges of the wreath. Fill in between these clusters with small bunches of another flower or herb. Add another flower on the face of the wreath, interspersed with yet another flower or herb. (Some may be easier to secure with floral wire or U-shaped pins.) Distribute colors and textures in a

As a variation on the wreath shape, try making a straight braid out of raffia grass. As you braid the raffia, work in dried herbs and flowers; use a hot glue gun to secure the dried plants if necessary. Glue on cloves of garlic and chili peppers to make a unique gift for a kitchen shower or housewarming.

pleasing arrangement; fill in any gaps with single flowers. Also add a bow, if you like.

A variation of this style is to choose one flower to be your background. (In the Old Fashioned recipe, for instance, artemesia would make a good choice.) Attach your background material first, clustering several short sprigs and attaching them with hot glue, U-shaped pins or florist picks. Work in the same direction all the way around so that everything points the same way. Scatter your accent flowers evenly throughout the wreath, and finish with a bow, if you want.

A few examples of "recipes" for wreaths follow, but you can make up your own using colors that coordinate with the recipient's taste in flowers, or decor.

Romantic	*Kitchen*
Lavender	Anise
Tansy	Basil
Rose yarrow	Dill
Golden yarrow	Parsley
Baby's breath	Tarragon
Santolina	Oregano
Mint	Thyme
Hydrangea	Garlic
Blue statice	Sage
White statice	Marjoram
Pink rosebuds	Red peppers (see the
Yellow rosebuds	photo on page 25)

Old Fashioned

Apples (see the photo on page 24)

Artemesia	
Astilbe	*Unusual*
Tansy	Rosemary
Teasel	Yarrow
Yarrow	Rabbit tobacco
Lunaria	Golden rod
Oregano flowers	Pinecones
Strawflowers	Siberian seedpods
Baby's breath	Button stems
	Cinnamon sticks

Apple Wreath: To make the apple wreath pictured on page 24, designed by Debbie Vitkow Davidson, begin by drying some apples. To dry apples, slice them ¼-inch thick, then place them in a baking dish and cover with 2 cups of lemon juice mixed with 3 tablespoons salt. Allow the apples to soak for 20 minutes, then blot them dry with a towel and place them on a baking rack. Put the apples in a 150 degree oven for 6 hours. (Store the lemon juice mixture in the refrigerator; it can be reused.) Remove the apples and allow them to cool before giving them at least two good coats of acrylic matte finish.

Weave eucalyptus around a wire wreath frame and glue it in place or attach it with floral wire. Tuck white statice sprigs in the wreath here and there to make it fuller and to add contrast. Lay the dried apples on top of the eucalyptus, then put dollops of hot glue in those spots and press the apples down into them. Fill in the areas between the apples with cinnamon sticks and whole nutmegs. Tie on a raffia bow for an accent, and attach a loop of wire on the back for hanging.

Making a Tussie Mussie

To create a tussie mussie, you'll make several tiny bouquets; then you'll wire them together into one. Use at least three different kinds of flowers; for instance, pink star flowers, purple statice, white gypsophilia, and one red clover. You can gather flowers from your garden or the wild and dry them, or you can buy them already dried.

Make bouquets with one or two center flowers (say, purple statice), surrounded by the bulk flowers (star flowers), with accent flowers (gypsophilia) tucked at three or four spots on the perimeter of the bouquet. Bind all these flowers together with floral wire; trim stems. Repeat.

Place a single flower (red clover) in the center of all the clustered bouquets, then wire the bunches together. Next, dye a doily to match your bouquet and/or package by "painting" it with wet tissue paper of the proper color. (See page 113 for more on this technique.) When the doily dries, wrap it around the bottom of the bouquet to cover the florist wire. Glue the doily in place, then bind with colored ribbon. Or, you could omit the doily and use lots of ribbon.

Making a Topiary

You can gather flowers from your garden or the wild and dry them, or buy them already dried for your topiary tree. Use at least three different kinds, and aim for pleasing relationships of color and shape. Trim flowers from their stems and arrange them by type

and color within easy reach.

Protect your work area with newspaper, and plug in your hot glue gun. Use the point of a scissors to poke a hole in a Styrofoam ball. Then push a stick into this hole and twist, gouging deeper into the Styrofoam. Remove the stick for now. With florist pins (or with a stapler opened up so it will staple flat), attach Spanish or sphagnum moss to the ball. Cover everything but the hole with moss.

Place some floral foam in the bottom of the flowerpot. As you did with the Styrofoam ball, poke a hole in the center of the foam with the scissors, then use the stick to push all the way through. Remove the foam and squirt some hot glue in the bottom of the flowerpot, then replace the foam. Glue the larger end of the stick into the hole in the foam. Glue several small rocks on top of the foam to help weight the topiary so it won't tip. Glue the moss covered Styrofoam ball onto the end of the stick.

Starting at the top of the Styrofoam ball, begin hot gluing flowers in place. Create a balanced arrangement here at the top of all the different kinds of flowers you're working with. You'll follow this pattern loosely as you move around the ball. If you have an extremely limited amount of any particular flower, you may want to go ahead and glue those blossoms on now, to make sure you get an even distribution. Conversely, if you have an abundance of some kind of flower, use it to fill in the gaps between the "featured" flowers. Don't forget to tip the topiary over and cover the bottom as well. When the ball is covered with flowers, arrange florist's grass to cover the foam and rocks in the flowerpot. Ribbons can be tied on the stick for an even dressier presentation.

Making Potpourri

There are many potpourri recipes that date back at least several centuries and still make good scents for rooms, closets and drawers. The basic formula is to use 1 tablespoon of spice (or a few drops of an essential oil) per 4 cups dried flowers; adding a fixative such as tincture of benzoin or orris root will make your mixture last a lot longer. Some commonly used flowers are roses, lavender, lemon verbena, scented geranium, rosemary, marjoram, marigolds and pansies.

Here's a woodsy recipe to try: In a ceramic bowl or other nonmetal container, crush and mix together

2 cups pine needles, 2 cups cedar chips, and 1 cup rosemary. Stir in 1 cup clover blossoms, 1 cup rosehips, 1 cup miniature pinecones, thirty dried cardamon seeds, 1 tablespoon whole cloves, and 1½ tablespoons orris root. Mix well and place in a glass container for several weeks; shake frequently to let the scents mix evenly.

For a floral scent, try mixing ½ cup each of rose geranium leaves and crushed lemon verbena with 1½ cups crushed lavender blossoms and 2 tablespoons calamus root.

Suppliers of Potpourri Ingredients

Lavender Lane, P.O. Box 7265, Citrus Heights, CA 95621 (catalog, $2).

Rosemary House, 120 S. Market St., Mechanicsburg, PA 17055 (catalog, $2).

Indiana Botanic Gardens, P.O. Box 5, Hammond, IN 46325.

Giving Live Plants

Potting Soil Mixtures: Most plants you'll give as gifts will grow happily in a standard potting soil mix. But cacti want sandy, well drained soil, and herbs develop stronger flavors if they're grown in poor soil, without fertilizers. Nurseries and plant stores sell special mixes for different types of plants, including African violets, philodendrons and cacti.

Winter Bulbs: If you follow directions carefully, it's easy to force spring bulbs for a live wintertime bouquet. Each flower has its own requirements, but daffodils and hyacinths share many characteristics. Plant these bulbs in early October in a decorative bowl or half pot. The pointed tips of the bulbs should poke up out of the potting soil. Place the pot in a dark, cool place for four to six weeks for hyacinths, and six to eight weeks for daffodils. This allows the roots to develop. (They need temperatures between 55 and 60 degrees.) After the roots have formed, the pots should be moved gradually into the sunlight to develop leaves and flowers. Talk to someone at your local nursery, or check a gardening book, for more specific information. These "uncut bouquets" make perfect gifts for mothers, mothers-in-law and good friends.

Since you gather the sticks yourself, a log cabin planter costs next to nothing to make. The only supplies you need, besides the twigs, are some small nails and a hammer. Yet this simple gift is appreciated by everyone with a taste for things rustic and outdoorsy, and anyone who likes a country or primitive style. It can be used indoors to hold houseplants or outdoors on the patio to corral summer blooms. (For instructions on how to make log cabin planters and end tables, see "Rustic Home Accessories," pages 39-40.)

Working With Found Materials

You can create unique rustic gifts for the nature lovers on your list. Some of the most charming gifts cost only pennies to make, using sticks, pinecones and other found materials. Note: If you gather materials yourself, eliminate bugs and other critters by baking your materials in a 200 degree oven for 30 minutes.

Twig Planters: Planters wrapped with twigs, vines or jute make unusual gifts. Save cuttings pruned from trees and bushes, or gather sticks that have fallen to the ground. Look for twigs that are fairly straight and of a similar thickness. Trim them to the height of your planter base (a 5-pound coffee can works well).

Paint the planter or coffee can a dark color in case any of its surface shows through the wrapping materials. Once the paint dries, place the can on its side and use a glue gun to attach sticks. You may have to pile several sticks on top of each other to completely cover the can. When you've worked all the way around, wrap the can with vines or jute; tie, then glue the vines or jute in place. Place a dried flower arrangement or a potted plant inside the can and tie a big bow on it. Or wrap the can with some tissue paper or clear oyster paper. (See the photo on page 21 for an example.)

Rustic Home Accessories: Log-cabin style centerpieces, plant stands and end tables are quick and easy to build. Gathering the sticks is fun, too—most can be cut with garden shears. All your sticks should be about the same size—carry a "measuring stick" with you and cut sticks to the proper size as you gather them.

To make an end table, use about forty-four 20-inch twigs (a ½- to ¾-inch diameter works well). Select two twigs of uniform size for the bottom. They should be as flat as possible—sand the bottoms if necessary to ensure stability. Then, place two more twigs perpendicularly on top of the first two, allowing a 1-inch overlap on the sides. Use a small flat-headed nail to hold the twigs in place. Repeat this process of placing two twigs on top of the preceding twigs, log-cabin style, until you've reached the desired height. Make a top for the table by laying twigs across the top, no more than ¼ inch apart, then nailing them in place. The table can be used as is, or topped with a piece of ¼-inch glass with polished edges.

To force an amaryllis bulb, plant it indoors in a pot in November or December. Keep it in a cool dark place for four to six weeks to root, then gradually move it into the sunlight so the plant can develop leaves and top growth. In another four to six weeks, gigantic amaryllis blossoms will appear.

To make a rustic plant stand or centerpiece, you'll use the same process, but with a bottom instead of a top. And instead of a square "log cabin" you'll be creating a rectangle, so gather sticks of two lengths—long ones for the sides, and shorter ones for the ends. Use long ones for the bottom, which will be assembled once the sides are made. This log cabin "box" can be used to hold live or dried plants, as a decorative container or as a centerpiece. Note: Pots need to be set in saucers, or you'll make a mess when you water the plants. An alternative would be to line the plant stand with a plastic trough, available at garden stores.

Pinecone Frame: With the same technique described for baskets in Chapter Two, you can make a unique frame for small prints. Purchase pinecones or gather them yourself, then glue them to an old frame that's been painted dark brown or black, just in case any of it shows through. A glue gun works particularly well, but it's not required. Some people prefer to use smaller pinecones of a nearly uniform size on frames. If you're working with different sizes, begin by gluing the larger ones in place, then fill in the gaps with medium and small ones. Continue adding pinecones until the frame is covered. (See photo on page 16.)

Pinecone Wreath: Wire pinecones onto a wire or Styrofoam base. Use all one kind, or mix a variety of shapes and sizes. Also include seeds and pods like buckeyes, walnuts, pecans, anise stars, honey locust pods and acorns. Add a bow and some dried statice or sprigs of evergreen, and you'll have a beautiful winter wreath. These also make beautiful centerpieces, with candles set in the middle.

Cinnamon Sticks: Though you can't gather these in the wild, they're as easy as pinecones to work with and are relatively inexpensive, especially during the holiday season. Hot glue cinnamon sticks onto a variety of surfaces: boxes, cans, desk accessories, ornaments and vases as well as using them as accents in wreaths, topiaries and potpourri.

Pressed Leaves: You can press leaves like flowers, as previously described, but it's okay to collect them when wet; simply blot between layers of paper towel to absorb the moisture. The key is to gather leaves when they're freshly fallen. To press, place them between layers of blotting paper, then newspaper, and weigh everything down with heavy books. If they've already turned color, they should only take about two weeks to press; otherwise, give them about a month. Use them soon after, though, or they'll get brittle and difficult to work with.

Another method is one many of us remember from elementary school: iron the leaves between waxed paper. Remove the leaf, let it cool, and press it overnight in a book. This technique works with green grasses and ivy, too.

You can use pressed leaves on a variety of projects, from framed collages to recipe boxes. Simply coat the undersides of the leaves with acrylic polymer medium, sold in art stores, and allow it to dry. Coat the object as well, then lay the leaves on the wet medium, which will act as your glue. Press the leaves down firmly with your fingertips, adding more polymer medium as necessary. Overlap the leaves for complete coverage. As you finish a section, lay scrap paper over it and press with a warm iron to help the leaves adhere. Just make sure there's not excess medium on top of the leaves, or the paper will stick!

When the object dries, give it a coat of varnish. When this dries, varnish again. Repeat until the leaves are completely covered.

FOUR

GIFTS OF FABRIC MAGIC

abric is a flexible medium that offers a wide range of gift possibilities. You can make wearables—everything from evening gowns to baby clothes—home accessories like lamp shades and duvet covers, and other miscellaneous gifts ranging from covered photo albums, picture frames and padded hangers, to toys, dolls and stuffed animals. Scraps of fabric can be used to make a variety of unique patchwork gifts: throw pillows, wall hangings, place mats and quilts. If you do needlework—embroidery, needlepoint, knitting or crocheting—this opens up even more possibilities.

This chapter is not just for people who sew, however, because there are also plenty of ideas for decorating ready-made projects. Try sewing antique doilies onto pillows you've purchased, or cut stamps from potatoes and dip them in fabric paints to decorate T-shirts. You can tie-dye or batik unique outfits. And, there are photo transfer mediums sold at craft stores which enable you to transfer photographs to T-shirts, pillows and more. You can even braid a rag rug or a set of place mats from leftover fabrics.

The How-To section at the end of this chapter provides easy step-by-step instructions for batik, and potato and other printing techniques. You'll also find

tips on tie-dyeing, braiding rags for rugs and place mats, and instructions on how to appliqué.

IDEAS

Because fabric presents so many possibilities, you'll need to use your imagination when reading the following list. Each of my ideas can be interpreted in a vast array of ways, so think hard about the person you intend to give the gift to, and what he or she seems to like most. (Refer to the quiz in Chapter One to help you get a vision of someone's taste and style.)

When giving a gift of clothing, be sure it's the right size. Also think about the colors a person wears most, and what he or she looks best in. Clothing style is also important—you wouldn't want to give a hand-painted T-shirt to a man who never wears T-shirts! And, when giving a home accessory as a gift, always consider the recipient's decor, color scheme and tableware.

Photo Albums, Picture Frames, Bandboxes and Blank Books: Add your own unique fabric covers to picture frames, bandboxes, store-bought blank books or photo albums. This can be as simple as gluing on a colorful chintz, or as elaborate as padding the cover and loading it with lace, ruffles and novelties. There are commercial patterns available for covering a variety of home accessories, or you can create your own. Just coat your box or frame with glue, then smooth fabric over it. For an extra touch, cover the object with wadding or fiberfill before topping with fabric, then finish with ribbon trims. Instructions for covering a photo album follow; see Chapter Seven, page 117, for complete instructions on covering bandboxes.

To cover a photo album, first remove the pages. Then, place the opened album on the wrong side of the fabric. Cut the fabric about 2 inches from the edges on all sides. If you want a padded cover, place the album on a sheet of cotton batting; cut the batting to the exact size of the album. Glue the batting to the outside of the album, then put the open album back down on the wrong side of the fabric.

Whether you used batting or not, your next step is to pull the fabric tightly around the album and tuck in the inside corners; hold it in place temporarily with Bulldog clips. Secure both sides of the spine, top and bottom, with clips, making sure that the fabric is tight, but that the book can be opened and shut eas-

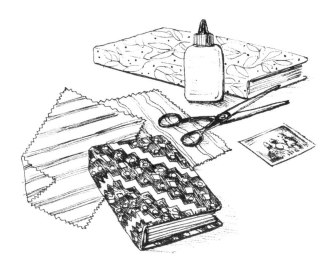

An album with some snapshots you've taken over the years or a fabric frame for a cherished family photo both make wonderful gifts for your parents—and your kids! It's easy to give boxes, frames and photo albums a designer treatment with colorful fabric. Simply coat the book or frame with glue, then smooth fabric over it.

Gifts for baby range from wall hangings, like this one painted
by Linda Konowal, to baskets (by Debbie Vitkow Davidson),
and photo albums such as this one made by Patty Knapp and
her sister Barbara Brown. (See page 42-44 for instructions.)

ily. Hot glue along the outside edges of the album and turn the excess fabric under. Trim the fabric at the corners of the album diagonally to about ½ inch; glue down the fabric allowance on the inside cover.

To make "endpapers" for the inside of the cover, cut two pieces of poster board, one for the front and one for the back, slightly smaller than the album cover. Cut the fabric slightly larger than the poster board and glue the fabric on; pull excess fabric to the back and glue down the edges. If you want the album to have lacy borders, glue your lace to the inside cover now, so it peeks over the edge of the cover slightly. Next, glue your poster board endpapers into the front and back inside covers of the album. Replace the pages.

If you want to make a "frame" for the front of the album (as illustrated in the photo on page 43), cut out a square of poster board. Trace a circle in the center by drawing around a mug or jar lid; cut this out. Repeat the process of covering the poster board with batting and fabric, as just described; glue on an edging of lace if desired. Then place the frame on top of the covered album and glue down three sides,

leaving the top open so a photo can be inserted.

Hostess Aprons and Potholders: Next time you need a gift for a hostess, instead of the same old bottle of wine everyone always brings, why not try something different? A hand-painted or batiked hostess apron makes a special statement, and matching potholders give it even more pizzazz. Commercial patterns give instructions for making everything from oven mitts, appliance covers and aprons, to cushions, chair covers and tablecloths. Or create a pattern using one of your aprons or oven mitts as a guide and adding seam allowances.

Wine Bottle Covers: If time is short and you opt to give a bottle of wine to your hostess after all, you can stitch up some unique gift wrap in under an hour. Simply make a tube by folding an 11 × 14-inch piece of cloth in half lengthwise, right sides together. If possible, cut your fabric so the selvage falls on one of the 11-inch sides. You can use this for the top, otherwise you'll need to sew a tiny hem in the top, or iron it in place with fusible web. Stitch up the side, then use a doubled thread to loosely stitch all the way around the bottom. Pull those threads tight; knot.

To make a pouch for an 8 × 5-inch notepad lay the fabric face down. Fold the 4½-inch piece onto the inside back to form a large hem. Next, fold the two back pieces together to form a pocket, as illustrated. The fabric should be inside out. Stitch up the sides, then turn right side out. Hem the sides of the front flap, if desired, or fray the unfinished edge artfully. Insert the notepad, flipping the front cover into position.

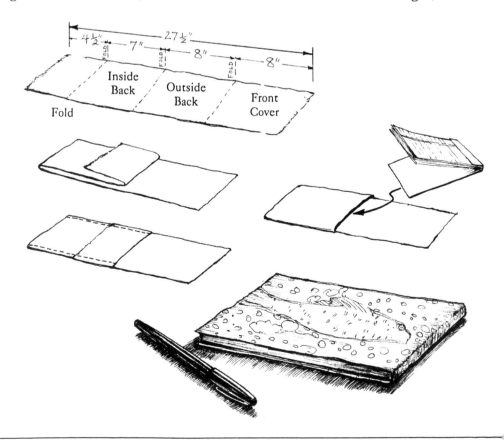

Turn the cover right side out, insert the bottle of wine, tie the top with a ribbon, or make a little tie out of fabric by stitching up a long, slender tube (right sides together, wrong side out) and sewing one end. Turn it right side out using a stick or a wooden spoon handle to push out the fabric.

Jar Lid Covers: Lid covers are a great way to put a final personalizing touch on such gifts as preserves or home-canned goodies. The simplest version is to cut a square from gingham or calico with pinking shears; more elaborate jar lid covers might be painted or even cross-stitched.

Notepad Covers: These spiffy little covers can be practically mass produced, so they're great for the holidays, when you need gifts for neighbors and for people at the office. You can make reusable notebook covers out of pretty fabric, or decorate fabric yourself using such techniques as fish printing, batiking and potato printing. See the illustration on page 44 for instructions on how to make a cover.

Table Ensembles: Place mats, napkins, table runners and tablecloths can be decorated in a variety of ways. They can be painted, batiked, stenciled, appli-quéd, embroidered, potato printed, spatter painted, or reverse dyed (bleached). Or, you can sew these home accessories out of calico, floral prints, bandanas, patchwork—you can even make mini "braided rugs" to use for place mats and coasters. Matching napkins and place mats make good presents at showers, birthdays and housewarmings; they can also be tucked into a gourmet or picnic gift basket, as shown in the photo on page 12.

Throw Pillows: Pillows can be decorated with patchwork, needlepoint, embroidery, batik, potato print or painted silk. Or create a collage of fabrics on a pillow using fusible web. Cut out geometric shapes of different colored cloth, or various motifs printed on different fabrics (different flowers, animals, designs, etc.). Follow the directions on the fusible web to attach these designs to your pillow fabric. Or try cutting and sewing fabric scraps together in an interesting pattern for an authentic patchwork pillow. You could batik a fish print on fabric (see page 57) and make a pillow (page 78). Resists and silk paints can also be used to create a beautiful picture on a pillow. (Also see the following on creating pillows with lace.)

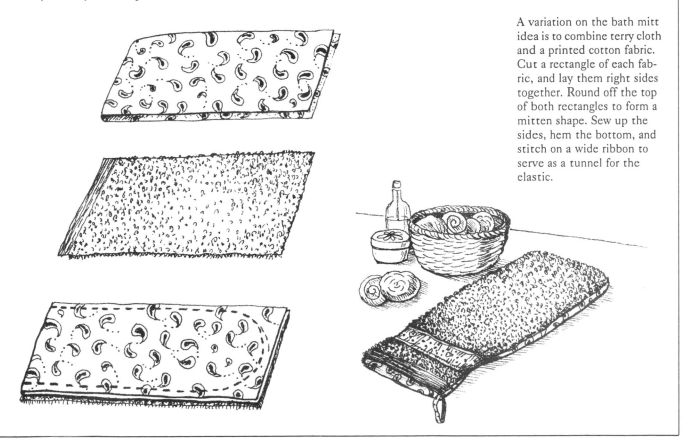

A variation on the bath mitt idea is to combine terry cloth and a printed cotton fabric. Cut a rectangle of each fabric, and lay them right sides together. Round off the top of both rectangles to form a mitten shape. Sew up the sides, hem the bottom, and stitch on a wide ribbon to serve as a tunnel for the elastic.

Flowers of all sorts make great gifts. Debbie Vitkow Davidson
made this hanging rose sachet by placing rose petals between
two circular pieces of lace. She held the lace together by
stretching it over an embroidery hoop, then used hot glue to
attach a ruffle around the outside edge. Debbie made the
bath basket, too, using "lilies of the valley" as a theme. For
color accents, she stuck small squares of colored tissue paper
around the rim. The barrettes were made by hot gluing dried
flowers onto plastic barrettes.

Floral-print fabrics can be used for lots of gift ideas. For instance, it's easy to cover an old hatbox with fabric. Other gift ideas pictured here include a basket painted and then embellished with fusible webbed fabric, and sachets to be tucked in drawers and hung in closets—some are pretty enough to hang on doorknobs!

Gifts of Old Lace: Many exquisite examples of antique handwork are gathering dust in drawers because people are afraid they'll wear out or be damaged. But these delicate heirlooms can be displayed in ways that also make great gifts for family members (and of course that includes *you!*). If you have old lace antimacassars (which were used to protect the backs and arms of chairs from men's hair oil), doilies, table runners, even antique gloves, consider sewing them onto a pillow (see photo on page 78).

Another option is to sew the lace item onto a piece of contrasting fabric, then frame it. Background fabric possibilities range from red velvet or blue satin to black canvas or sailcloth. Yet another idea involves hand coloring the flowers or other designs on the doily with fabric paints before sewing it onto a backing or a pillow. If you weren't lucky enough to inherit antique doilies, purchase new ones at a craft or department store or scout secondhand shops for old ones.

Buttons Galore: As with old lace, there are a lot of antique buttons hanging around in sewing boxes. The fanciest might be best used in jewelry (see Chapter Six), but more run-of-the-mill buttons can be

Canvas bags are simple to make, or you can decorate store-bought versions. Decorate plain bags using leaf prints, stencils, potato prints or batik. You might embellish a bag with ribbons, lace and buttons, or use no-sew appliques and dimensional fabric paints.

used to decorate everything from sweatshirts, satchels and shoulder bags to pillows, headbands and sachets. Sew buttons in a swirling pattern around the neck and cuffs of a sweatshirt, for instance, or decorate a heart sachet with some of your grandma's treasured buttons.

Handkerchiefs: Old hankies can be used to make sachets, pillows, even a curtain or tablecloth! Because they're so delicate, they need to be sewn to an interfacing or backing material with invisible nylon thread or tiny running stitches. A tablecloth requires quite a few handkerchiefs, but if you collect them over time at garage sales and flea markets, it will be a wonderful present for a bride. Use fine muslin as a backing, and lay the hankies in a pleasing arrangement, overlapping them if you like. Pin them in place, then hand stitch them with invisible thread. You may want to let some of the hankies fall partly off the muslin to create a softer, romantic border.

Sachets: Stitch up little hearts, or even just little squares of pretty fabric, and fill them with potpourri (see Chapter Three for recipes and basic instructions). As an extra touch, embellish your sachet with trims of lace or ribbon. Or sew on loops of ribbon (as pictured on page 47), so the sachet can be hung on a hanger in the closet, or even dangled from a chair arm or doorknob as a decorative accent.

Bath Mitt: A bath mitt makes a great gift in combination with some fancy soap. You can make a handy mitt out of a couple of hand towels, mix two fabrics — some scraps of terry cloth and a cotton print, for instance. Cut two rectangles, about 6 × 12 inches, and lay them right sides together. Sketch a rounded mitten shape at one end of the rectangle, then cut away the top of both pieces to conform with this shape. Sew the mitt together, then zigzag or overstitch the outside edges of the seam to prevent raveling. Hem the bottom edge, if necessary, then turn the mitt right side out. Sew on a wide piece of ribbon or sturdy facing about 1½ inches from the bottom edge to serve as a tunnel for the elastic. Thread the elastic through; stitch the ends in place. See page 45.

Hand Towels: Paint a folksy scene or print a wild design around the bottom of a hand towel. (Look for those that have a smooth, tightly woven strip near the bottom to facilitate your creative process.) Any acrylic paint will work, as long as you heat set it, so a vast array of colors is available. These towels make great housewarming or shower gifts.

Padded Hangers: Give a set of padded hangers to your favorite clotheshorse. Use fabric scraps or decorate fabric yourself with paints, batik or stamping techniques. To begin, purchase wooden hangers, measure them, then stitch up tubes of fabric long enough to encase the hangers, leaving an opening in the middle of one side. Stuff the tubes with fiberfill or potpourri (see Chapter Three for recipes) after sliding them onto the hangers, then stitch up the opening.

Pillowcases and Sheets: Sheets seem an ambitious undertaking because they're so large, but remember, you only have to decorate the top edge, especially if you purchase colorful bed linens. Sheets and pillowcases can be sponge painted, printed, embroidered, hand painted, appliquéd, even batiked. They make a nice wedding shower or housewarming gift, while colorfully decorated crib sheets would make a charming baby shower gift.

Baby Clothes: For showers and birthdays, clothes make great gifts for babies. If you sew, you can make them yourself—for instance, an easy project is a "designer" bib. Cut out different kinds of material and appliqué little suits for boys, using different fabrics to look like a vest and a white shirt with little buttons. Calico and lace creations are great for little girls. Bibs might be painted with animal faces or stamped with overall patterns; fish prints also look great on bibs. Baby clothes are small, so they're much quicker to decorate than adult clothes; they can be an effective way of testing out new ideas. Buy a pack of tiny T-shirts, a bonnet or a romper suit, and create your own unique brand of kid chic.

Stuffed Animals: Handmade toys will be cherished for a lifetime. Pattern companies offer a variety of designs for stuffed animals and rag dolls, or you can create your own, tailor-made to the child's taste. Simple animal shapes can be painted on fabric, then sewn together like a pillow. Finger puppets and bean bags are also easy and fun to make.

Tennis Shoes: These make great gifts for kids. Buy canvas or leather sneakers or spruce up old shoes. (Be sure to wash canvas shoes before painting.) Sketch out your design ideas on paper first, using markers to color them. Then transfer a rough outline of your design to the shoes. Paint the canvas with colorful fabric paints or markers. For fun, paint or buy wild laces to match.

Headbands, Bracelets and Ponytail Holders: Good for putting in bath baskets, these accessories also make great stocking stuffers. Sew a tube of cloth or ribbon, right sides together. Make it extra long so it bunches up when you thread elastic through it. (A typical headband is about 24 inches long; a bracelet, 13 inches; a pony tail holder, 7 inches.) Turn it right side out and thread elastic through. Sew the ends of the elastic together; turn a tiny bit under and stitch a blind seam.

Silk Scarves: Silk looks stunning when painted; using a resist technique will help you control the color. (See the How-To section for detailed instructions.) And not only can a scarf be worn, some of them are so beautiful they deserve to be framed.

Clothes: If you sew, you can create unique designer garments for family and friends. But even if you don't, you can buy ready-made clothes and decorate them. Sponge and spatter painting are quick and easy ways to provide an overall pattern, but don't forget appliqué—it's a snap with fusible web! You can cut pictures or patterns from commercial cloth, and fuse them to a blouse or dress with a minimum of sewing. (See Easy Appliqué—Working With Fusible Web in the How-To section, page 64.)

Sweatsuits and Other Outfits: There are so many ways to decorate sweatsuits that you should have no problem tailoring one exactly to the recipient's taste. Just for starters, consider the following products: acrylic fabric paints, dimensional fabric paints, spray webbing, fusible web and fabric, and photo transfers. And don't forget techniques such as potato print, batik, tie-dye and spatter paint. If the person you're making a gift for doesn't wear sweatsuits, consider decorating another kind of outfit, like a shorts set or a skirt and blouse.

T-Shirts: T-shirts make great gifts for kids and teenagers. Just like sweatsuits, T-shirts can be painted with dimensional paints, potato printed, stamped with leaves or fish, batiked, hand painted, marbleized . . . Let your imagination run wild! Note: When painting T-shirts, be sure to insert a large piece of cardboard in the shirt, or a special cardboard T-shirt form available at craft stores, to prevent the

Laura Bolt handpainted the T-shirt (shown folded) to look like a cut paper design by Matisse, making it a perfect gift for art lovers. Maya Contento made the shirt with grapes, which she calls "Fruit on the Vine." For visual interest, she applied more than one color to each stamp, and varied the colors every time she repainted a stamp. Maya will testify that decorated T-shirts make great gifts. She started out potato printing shirts as gifts for friends, but her creations were so popular they turned into a business.

Braided rugs transform old clothes into handmade gifts. To make this rug, I tore up three dresses, four shirts, two pillowcases, several ties, a denim jumpsuit and one nightgown. You can also purchase fabric remnants in complementary colors and braid with them.

paint from bleeding through onto the back.

Bags and Carryalls: A lot of people love big cloth bags—women use them when traveling, or to schlepp special projects around town; students use them as book bags; and the ecologically minded take them grocery shopping. Bags are simple to make out of canvas, or you can buy them ready-made and decorate them. Stencils work well to decorate with, as do potato prints; you can even sew on ribbons and lace, and of course, appliqué.

To make a stencil, draw a simple design on a piece of cardboard. Use a mat knife or an X-Acto to cut out your stencil, then place it on the flattened bag. (Iron the bag first, if necessary.) Use a stencil brush or a sponge to apply paint within the cutout. Carefully lift off your stencil, and repeat in another area. You may want to turn your stencil, or even flip it over, to create an interesting varied pattern.

Braided Rag Rugs and Place Mats: These homey gifts evoke the simple pleasures of a bygone era. Handmade rugs help create a cozy atmosphere, a downhome feeling of old-fashioned hospitality. They're easy to make, though they always seem to

require more fabric than you expect. You can use scraps and rags you have on hand, or buy remnant yardage in coordinated colors. Also, you can use the same plaiting technique to make place mats and coasters. (See the How-To section for more details.)

Patchwork Quilts: Although this doesn't qualify as a quick gift, if you dispense with hand sewing and work on the machine, it cuts down your time investment considerably. Quilts were popular in the past because they provided not only warmth, but color and beauty. Designs composed of strips or squares are easiest to put together, but experienced quilters can piece together all manner of unique designs. In the old days, many patchwork quilts were made from clothes that could no longer be worn; calico was the supreme material.

Quilts consist of three parts: the quilt top, or pattern, often patchwork, composed of a series of squares; the lining, or the back, sometimes made of soft flannel; and the interlining, sandwiched between the top and the lining, usually made of cotton batting or sometimes an old blanket. These three layers are bound together by quilting—fine stitches in a variety

A carved potato and a bunch of celery can both be used to print unique designs on fabric or wrapping paper. See Printing Techniques, pages 53-60.

of patterns. Quilting is currently enjoying a revival. New books are coming out on the subject all the time. If you want to learn more about this homespun art, check your public library for specific titles.

Patchwork Pillows and Wall Hangings: You can give the beauty and color of a quilt without the bulky material and time investment. The fastest way to create either is to find an old quilt that's seen better days, then cut out blocks or squares that are still in good shape. Sew the blocks into pillow shapes and stuffed animals, or mount and frame the blocks. You can also make your own patchwork. Again, if you defy tradition and use machine stitching to quilt, you'll save a bundle of time.

Lamp Shades: Shades are a particularly good way to display batik because the light shines through to create a look similar to stained glass. Simply buy or salvage a wire lamp shade frame, then cut the batiked fabric so it overlaps both top and bottom by about an inch. Fold the edges under and pin them to the frame, then hand stitch the fabric into place using a simple running stitch.

You can also make rag rug style lamp shades using lengths of colored fabric. Tear the fabric into 3-inch wide strips, then weave the strips over and under the spokes of the shade. Tuck under the raw edges as necessary to hide fraying. When necessary, sew the ends together on the bias by placing the end of one strip on top of and perpendicular to another strip to create one continuous strip. (See the illustration for making braiding strips on page 63 for more information.) Conceal the top and bottom hoop by twisting folded strips around them.

Wreath of Fabric Scraps: These are quick, easy and inexpensive to make, and can have incredible variety depending on the fabric you use. For a baby shower, you might use pink and white with a teddy bear rattle; for Christmas, red and green with plaid ribbon. Or make a wild combination of different fabrics. To begin, use pinking shears to cut out 4 × 4-inch squares of cloth, then poke them into the wreath form with scissors and hot glue or U-shaped pins. Finish with a bow, a novelty item, or both.

HOW-TO'S

Even if you don't sew, try your hand at some of the following decorative techniques for fabric. You can create unique gifts of fabric without sewing a stitch. If you do sew, the sky's the limit!

Printing Techniques
What to print? There are literally hundreds of things you can decorate using a printing technique, including notepad covers, throw pillows, curtains, pillowcases and sheets, beanbags, stuffed animals and doll clothes, potholders, hostess aprons, tablecloths, place mats and napkins, baby and children's clothes, kimonos, blouses, dresses, skirts, shirts, T-shirts and exercise suits. You can also print such paper items as stationery and desk sets (blotter, pencil holder and notepad) as covered in Chapter Six. Here are a few suggestions for things to print *with*, multiplying your possibilities exponentially.

Leaf Prints: Try printing different leaves in a variety of fall colors on scarves, table runners and T-shirts; or print green leaves on a bright pastel fabric. First, collect freshly fallen leaves from your yard, or purchase them from a florist. Wash your fabric to remove the sizing before printing. Place a leaf on a paper plate and brush it with paint. Once it's completely covered, lay the leaf on your work surface, which has been protected with waxed paper or aluminum foil. Then, carefully lay the fabric or paper on top of the leaf. Use a rolling pin covered in plastic wrap or waxed paper to press the fabric down on the leaf; rub the fabric with your fingers to make sure the entire leaf print transferred. Lift up the fabric and pull the leaf loose. Hang the fabric or lay it flat to dry before printing the next leaf.

Celery Prints: Celery makes several different impressions. When you chop off the stalks and use a rubberband to hold them together at one end in a loose bouquet, celery makes a random pattern of rounded crescent shapes. When you stamp with the round bottom of the bunch, celery looks a lot like a cabbage rose. Printing with several different colors further expands the possibilities. Celery prints look great on T-shirts, sweatsuits and other clothing. You could even dye a shirt, and then batik on top of it. Celery prints are also a quick and easy way to decorate large home accessories such as sheets, tablecloths and curtains.

Textural Prints: Add texture to your fabric by printing it with burlap; also try feathers, paper doilies,

When it comes to clothing you can decorate, the possibilities are endless. You can paint on shorts sets and blouses, as shown here, as well as scarves, dresses, even ties. A shorts set might double as pajamas; this one was potato printed and dyed purple, then spots of red were added with a paint brush. For someone who doesn't wear T-shirts, how about a blouse that's stamped with the cut-off end of a bunch of celery, like the indigo one pictured here? The T-shirt in the back was batiked with a scene of Rio de Janerio. You can use the same idea to recreate all sorts of painted cities.

sea sponges, hardware, figurines and baskets. Fruits and vegetables, such as half a cabbage or half an orange, can also be printed. If you look around the house, you're sure to find all kinds of printing possibilities. (Remember that a water-based paint will wash off of objects if you clean it up immediately.) Print with anything: a piece of metal grillwork and the end of a bamboo brush, or a carved soapstone perfume jar. Even try things that you'd think wouldn't work. I made an "abstract expressionist" pillow printed with burlap and gypsophila flowers.

Sponge Prints: Purchase Miracle Sponges (which are thin and easy to cut) at a craft store, or use ordinary kitchen sponges or plastic foam meat trays to print different designs. Cut simple shapes like hearts, flowers and birds, or geometric shapes like circles, squares and triangles, and print clothes or home accessories with them.

Finger and Hand Prints: These prints look especially good on kids' clothing. Use your hand to make one or more hand prints, or make fingerprints and use them as the basis for cute little caricatures on T-shirts, tote bags and baby bibs. Add freehand details to your caricatures with a brush.

Photo Transfers: You can transfer your family photos onto clothing, T-shirts, pillows, sachets and doilies using a special medium. Some popular brands of photo transfer medium are Picture This, by Plaid Enterprises, and Second Impressions, by Delta. Check your craft store for others. Photo printed items make great gifts for family and friends. Both black-and-white and color photocopies will work; you can then embellish the pictures with fabric paints, lace, ribbons, trims or sequins to make unique gifts. Designs can be sentimental or campy, simple or ornate, depending on the pictures, colors and treatments you choose.

This process is simple, so you may want to do several T-shirts or pillows at once. Use 100 percent cotton or a polyester and cotton blend; be sure to prewash any new items to remove sizing. Make photocopies of the pictures you want to transfer. You can use a color photocopy of a stunning picture from a calendar, or a black-and-white copy of an heirloom photo of one of your ancestors. Also remember that you can use the reduction and enlargement features on the photocopy machine to enhance a layout. Fol-

Clothing can be tie-dyed for the more unconventional dressers on your list. The bottom of this summer T-shirt was twisted into a coil after rubber bands had been used to create a series of small circles on the top of it. (See the illustration on page 56 for some examples of the many ways tie-dye patterns can be produced.)

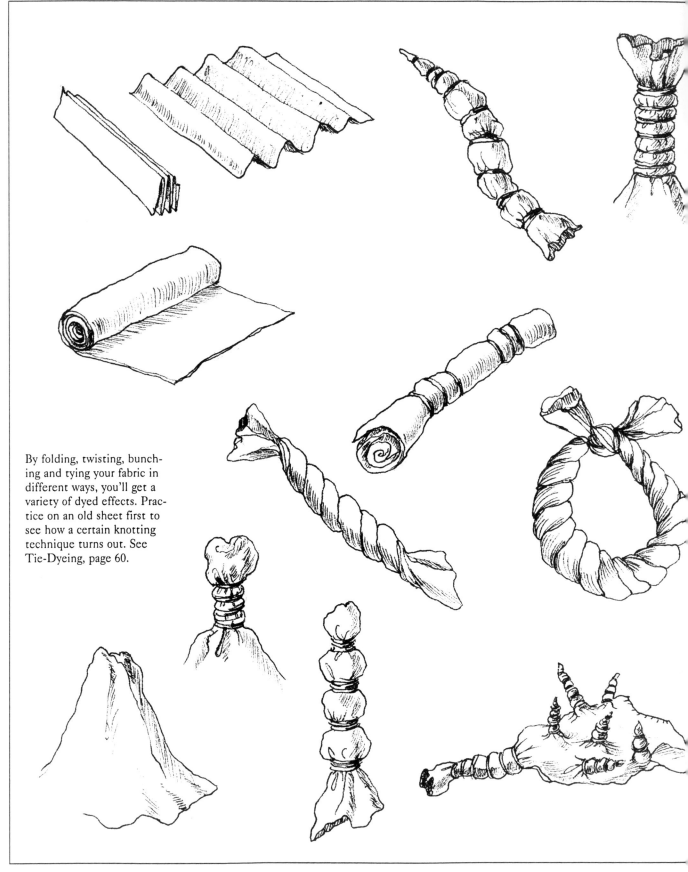

By folding, twisting, bunching and tying your fabric in different ways, you'll get a variety of dyed effects. Practice on an old sheet first to see how a certain knotting technique turns out. See Tie-Dyeing, page 60.

low manufacturer's directions to make the transfer. One word of caution: Fabrics with photo transfers need to be washed on a delicate cycle or by hand, and should never be put in the dryer!

Fish Printing

A fish-printed T-shirt, sweatshirt or fishing hat makes a great gift for anyone who's fascinated by fish. Adding impressions of sea fans and sponges along with a fish print creates a complete underwater picture. Or combine the fish print technique with batik for a really unique look.

You'll need a whole fish with scales (a sea bass works well), an old plate or some other palette, paintbrushes (including a stencil or other stubby, dense brush) and fabric paints. Sea fans (available at pet stores) and a sea sponge are optional. Fish prints can also be made on rice paper and framed. Just be sure to choose colors that will coordinate with the recipient's decor.

Step 1: To begin, cover your work surface with newspaper. Wrap a piece of cardboard with aluminum foil and place your fish in the center. Put a large dollop of fabric paint on your palette; don't thin it.

Step 2: You should practice on paper before trying to print a T-shirt. With a stencil brush (or some other short, densely bristled brush), paint the fish from head to tail, brushing in the direction of the scales. Then, carefully place a piece of scratch paper on top of the fish and rub, starting at the head. When you've covered the entire fish or can faintly see a full impression of the fish through the paper, pull off the paper. Try pulling another print before you reapply paint to see that effect. Then re-ink the fish and repeat. Be careful not to get paint on the cardboard the fish is resting on, as this can ruin the print. If you do get paint on the cardboard, slip a clean piece of paper under the fish before doing your rubbing.

When you feel comfortable and fairly in control of the technique, switch to your T-shirt or other item to be decorated. Put a piece of cardboard inside the shirt to make sure the paint doesn't penetrate to the back. If you want to print more than one fish, repeat as many times as you like.

Step 3: Once the fish prints are dry, you may want to add sponges and sea fans. Place a sheet of cardboard inside the T-shirt, then lay the sea fan down on top of the T-shirt, arranging it so that it frames the fish. Holding the fan firmly in place with one hand, load your stencil brush with paint. Jab the brush down lightly into the sea fan pattern. The sea fan itself creates a resist, and you can also choose not to paint certain areas, if you wish. Follow the natural vein line of the plant, and don't brush beyond it. When you've covered all the areas you want, move the sea fan to another spot and begin again. Play around with different mixtures of colors. Continue adding sea fans until you're satisfied with the design.

You can also make sea fan rubbings, as you did with the fish. In this case, you paint the sea fan, then press the fabric down on top of it and rub it to make sure the paint transfers. This method creates a more skeletal look than the soft fullness of the resist.

Step 4: To add a soft, blurry sea sponge, saturate a natural sponge with water and wring it out thoroughly. Put a small amount of paint on a plate and spread it around. Wipe the plate with the sponge then press it onto scratch paper. Repeat. Also try working with a dry sponge—it creates a much different look. When you're comfortable with the process, move to your T-shirt.

Step 5: Once the paint is dry—at least 24 hours— iron it to heat set the color. If you want to add yet another dimension, wax the entire shirt with paraffin, put it in the freezer so the wax cracks, then dip it in a dark blue dye. (See the instructions for batik that follow for more explicit directions.)

Potato Printing

Potato printing is an easy way to make beautiful, personalized gifts for all occasions. Using a stamping technique allows you to create an endless array of unique clothing and home accessories in a fraction of the time they would take to paint. Potatoes can be carved into recognizable shapes, like flowers or animals, or they can simply be used to create a pattern.

You'll need a surface to print on, potatoes, a sharp pencil, an X-Acto or paring knife, china plate or palette, paper towels, ruler, scratch paper for practice, and paints. Play with your designs on scrap paper before cutting your potatoes.

Step 1: Wash the fabric or ready-made clothing to remove any sizing. Dry and press.

Step 2: Slice potatoes in half lengthwise for large

It's easy to use a stencil to create a dramatic pattern on an article of clothing. For this kimono, I created a triangular shaped stencil to batik around. Then I cut out the fabric pieces and batiked them before sewing the garment. Paraffin provides the "crackled" look. (I was able to use straight paraffin instead of the usual fifty-fifty mix with beeswax, because I only did one dye dip.)

and medium shapes; slice in half widthwise for small ones. First trace your design on the potato with a pencil, then begin carving it. The key to carving potatoes is to think negatively: What you cut away will remain white, whatever surface is left will print your colors. Trim off the edges to avoid printing a characteristic "potato shape."

Step 3: Prepare your palette. Fabric paints are good, but any acrylic will work, as long as you heat set it by ironing. Use paints thick, just as they come from the jar, with a different brush for each color.

Step 4: Practice first on a large piece of scrap paper. Brush paint on the potato, put it down gently and press. If you aren't happy with a shape, re-cut parts of it or try again on another potato. Experiment by adding water to the paint to create soft blurry edges, but be sparse with your paint application. You can always re-stamp an area with more color, but a big glob of paint can ruin your design.

Step 5: Keep adding stamped images, working your way around the paper, developing the design all at once. Try to avoid symmetry — lining things up exactly on opposite sides of the center. Also, as you

work, turn the paper around so that you can see it from different angles.

Step 6: Finally, fill in the design with smaller stamps, working to create a balance between the elements. If possible, turn your stamps in different directions for variety. Once you've finished stamping, you may want to add small details such as stems and vein lines with the liner brush. Touch up areas that didn't quite print, add a highlight or overprint. Don't get too fussy, however; part of the appeal of this technique is its primitive look.

Step 7: When you're satisfied with your design, duplicate it on fabric. Draw light pencil guidelines if necessary; this can be helpful on place mats, for instance, where you'll be stamping within a defined border. Any pencil lines that aren't covered by paint will wash out. If you're working with a T-shirt or some other piece of clothing, place a piece of cardboard inside it to prevent the paint from bleeding through. Before you begin, dry your potatoes on a paper towel. (Otherwise, those overly wet stamps will create big blobs on your fabric.)

Step 8: If you don't finish your piece all in one

The tjanting is a tool used to "write" with hot wax. It produces beautiful, flowing lines and emphatic dots, and is great for adding details to a piece. Unless you don't care about wax getting on the back of the shirt, keep a piece of cardboard or a T-shirt form inside the shirt while you're working.

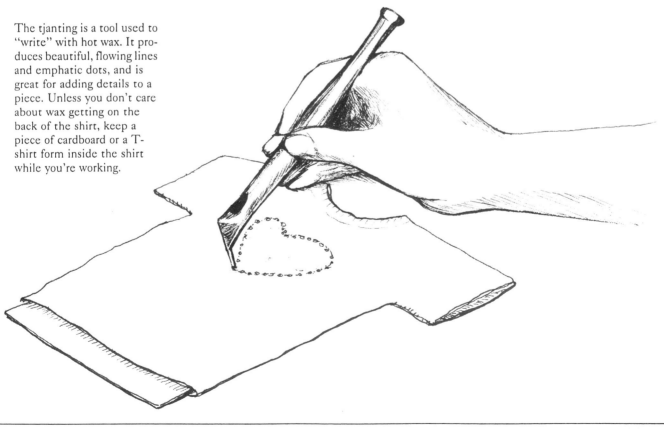

session, wash off your potatoes and save them. Carved potatoes will keep for about three days in the refrigerator if submerged in cold water and stored in an airtight plastic container. Before you use them, dry them off thoroughly with a paper towel.

Step 9: Many fabric paints don't require heat setting, but check the manufacturer's directions. Always heat set when in doubt—it can't hurt! (It also tends to make the paints softer, if they are stiff.) Simply iron the project, inside out. Once your project is finished, wait at least 48 hours before laundering it.

Tie-Dyeing

This is a simple resist method that uses tightly tied strings or rubber bands to prevent dye from being absorbed by fabric. Folding or twisting the fabric before tying it will also produce interesting effects. You can use commercial dyes sold in supermarkets, but natural fabrics work best. Tie-dye looks super on T-shirts, skirts, table accessories and scarves.

Step 1: Wash the items to be tie-dyed to remove sizing. You may want to experiment on fabric scraps before undertaking a large project.

Step 2: Pinch a section of cloth and bind it tightly with strings or rubber bands. To create a sunburst effect, bind another section beneath the first, then another (see the illustration on page 56). Continue binding sections of cloth with rubber bands for an overall pattern, or confine your knots to one section, such as the neckline, for an accent.

You might also try folding the garment, pleat-style, in straight lines, then securing it with rubber bands. Or you can do a simple running stitch, using strong thread, then pull the thread tight (gather it); next add rubber bands to bind more patterns into the gathers. Or, just twist the fabric into a coil, then bind it with rubber bands for a loose, textural design.

Step 3: If you want your design to feature several colors, you may want to paint one on. Mix a dye thickener, such as Rit's Design It or Superclear 100-N, with your desired shade of dye, then squirt it near and around the areas wrapped with rubber bands. When this dries, bind it with rubber bands to preserve that color. Repeat this process with other colors, if desired. Another option is to purchase special tie-dye cords that are already impregnated with dye.

Step 4: To get an overall color, you'll dip the entire piece in a dye bath. Use commercial dyes like Rit or Tintex, or Procion cold water dyes (described in the Batiking section in this chapter). Follow the manufacturer's directions; with commercial dyes, you'll get stronger colors if you heat the dye bath on the stove. Submerge the fabric in the dye bath and stir for half an hour or so; again, follow manufacturer's directions. Once the color is several shades darker than desired (it fades when it dries), remove the fabric from the dye and rinse it until the water runs clear. If you're only doing one color, remove the rubber bands and let the piece drip dry. If you plan to do another dip, or squirt on another color selectively, leave the rubber bands on.

Step 5: If you want to add another color, wrap rubber bands around the areas you want to remain the first color, then squirt or dip again. Remember, colors will combine to create a new color, so use those that will work together. Consult the Color Combination Chart on page 61 to get an idea of how this works.

Batiking

This ancient art form has a unique look. Its characteristic crackle and brilliant color can't be duplicated. Though it requires some special supplies, once you get started, you'll find it's easy and fun to do. Start with small items, like a pillow or a T-shirt. Later you may want to use a stencil to create an overall pattern on a tablecloth or a large article of clothing. For a one-color only design, batik with paraffin for lots of crackle. Tape the edges of the stencil with masking tape and wipe it often to prevent wax buildup.

Use 100 percent cotton—this can be a T-shirt, a dress, a pillowcase, yardage, anything—but be sure to wash it first to remove sizing, otherwise, the dyes won't take. Brushes will be full of hardened wax when you're done, so be willing to sacrifice them.

You'll also need a tjanting wax tool. It's shown on page 59. You can get it from a craft store or one of the suppliers listed on page 64. You'll also need paper to cover your work area, a sharp pencil, ruler, hotplate, beeswax, paraffin, a clean coffee can, an old pan, a piece of cardboard, scrap of fabric for practice, uniodized salt, washing soda, bucket, rubber gloves, sponge, measuring spoons, old jar with lid for dissolving dye, stick or old wooden spoon to stir the dye, hanger, brown paper bags, newsprint (or newspapers several months old) and an iron.

Finally, you need to use Procion cold water dyes to avoid melting the wax. These come in a rainbow of hues and are available at craft stores and from the suppliers on page 64. Don't use Tintex, Rit or other commercial dyes—they require hot water, which would melt your wax. Also, because batik requires multiple dips into different colors, you must plan your design so your colors will work together. See the following chart for help in mixing your colors.

Color Combination Chart

yellow + blue = green	green + blue = turquoise
yellow + red = orange	blue + orange = brown
red + blue = purple	orange + green = brown
red + green = brown	

Step 1: Wash your fabric to remove any sizing. Dry and press the fabric, then cover your work area with several layers of paper.

Step 2: Melt equal parts of beeswax and paraffin in a double boiler. Use an old pan for the boiling water and place the wax in a coffee can. (Wax is extremely flammable and under no circumstances should it be heated over direct flame! *Always* use a double boiler.) As the wax is melting, use a pencil to sketch out your design. Draw all the important lines; the rest of your design can be filled in freehand.

Step 3: When the wax in the coffee can is completely liquified, put the brush or the tjanting in and let it sit for a minute to heat. Then carefully fill the receptacle with melted wax, and use the tjanting like a pen on your scrap of fabric to get the feel of the tool. When you feel comfortable with the technique, slip the piece of cardboard into the T-shirt or other garment to keep the wax from seeping through to the back. (Unless your design is fairly abstract and you don't care about stray drops of wax.)

Remember that the places you put the wax will remain white, while the rest of the cloth will absorb the dye. Dip your tjanting in hot wax, and follow the penciled lines. If you have large areas that you want

When batiking, always use a double boiler to melt the wax. Find an old pan to use for the boiling water, and place the wax in a clean coffee can. When the wax is completely liquified, put the brush or the tjanting in and let it sit for a minute to heat. If using a tjanting, carefully fill the receptacle with melted wax. The tjanting may be used like a pen to draw fine lines and designs on your fabric, as shown on page 59.

to remain white, use a brush to apply wax to them.

Move your hand slowly but steadily across the fabric. The wax needs to go all the way through the fabric to prevent the dye from seeping in. If the wax is permeating the cloth it will look translucent. To be sure it's getting through, turn the piece over; if the wax is penetrating you'll see it on that side. If you don't see it, go ahead and wax that side too.

Next, use the tjanting to draw tiny wax lines and dots. Again, turn the piece over and wax that side too, if the wax doesn't penetrate. Remember that only the areas you wax will remain white. It's a good idea to wax more than you think you should—there always seems to be less of a color than envisioned, once a piece is dyed.

Step 4: Now you're ready for your first dye dip. Set up your dye bucket in the basement or bathtub; try to remove anything that would be damaged by a stray drop of dye. Wear rubber gloves and keep a sponge handy for cleaning up spills. Follow the manufacturer's instructions for mixing up the dye. Measure the dyestuff carefully and dissolve it in a jar of hot water before adding it to your bucket of cold water. Place the fabric in the dye bath; add a cup or so of uniodized salt dissolved in hot water; stir. Let sit at least thirty minutes and stir it occasionally to prevent uneven dye absorption.

Step 5: After the color is several shades darker than you want it, dissolve washing soda or soda ash in hot water, then add it to the dye bath. This will activate and fix the dye. Stir the mixture; allow it to soak for another twenty minutes or so. Then, take the fabric out of the dye bath and rinse it thoroughly with cold water. When the water runs clear, hang up your fabric to dry.

Step 6: Once the cloth is dry, repeat the waxing process, being sure the wax permeates the fabric. Again, it's wise to wax more than you think you need to; there always seems to be less color when the fabric dries. Repeat the dyeing process, this time with a dye bath of a second color. Remember that the colors must work together—check the chart on page 61 when in doubt.

Step 7: When the second dip is dry, repeat the entire process. Or if you want to get a lot of crackle in your background, melt pure paraffin in another coffee can. Use the brush to stroke paraffin all over the fabric until it's totally covered; turn it over and make sure the wax is permeating. Beeswax is flexible. It will bend without breaking—that's why it was used on the first two waxings, which need to withstand several dye dips. But paraffin is brittle; it breaks and falls off at the least provocation. The dye then permeates the cracks and influences your design in unexpectedly wonderful ways.

To help the paraffin's natural frailty along, crumple the waxed cloth into waves, and/or fold the entire thing in a pattern that complements your design. Then place it in a plastic bag in the freezer for at least 20 minutes. When you're ready to dye it, unfold it and crumple it again. The wax will flake off freely.

Repeat the dye bath process with another color. Rinse your fabric and let it dry—this won't take long because only the cracks were exposed.

Step 8: Once the cloth is dry, iron out the wax between old grocery bags or other nonprinted paper such as newsprint. (Newspapers are okay if they're more than two months old, otherwise the ink may come off on your fabric.) Keep ironing until the wax stops coming through the paper; then iron the cloth itself. Be sure to clean your iron off thoroughly before using it on real clothes! (I keep an old iron especially for ironing out batiks; look for a bargain at garage sales and thrift stores.) If you don't like the stiffness of the residual wax, take the piece to the dry cleaners and the fabric will be restored to normal again.

Other Resists

A resist is a colorless liquid. It hardens when applied to cloth, and is used to separate different areas, or colors, of a design. Resists are commonly used in silk painting. Painting with resists gives the same rich, "stained glass" look as batik, but it's less of a production since you aren't working with hot wax.

Step 1: Wash and dry your fabric first to remove sizing, then lightly pencil on your design. (If you're making an animal or doll, remember that you will sew *right* sides together, and make the back a mirror image shape of the front.)

Step 2: Using pushpins, stretch the fabric tightly across an old picture frame or stretcher bars. Use a resist medium to outline your design, making sure it penetrates the fabric and that your lines connect. Turn your project over and hold it up to the light to

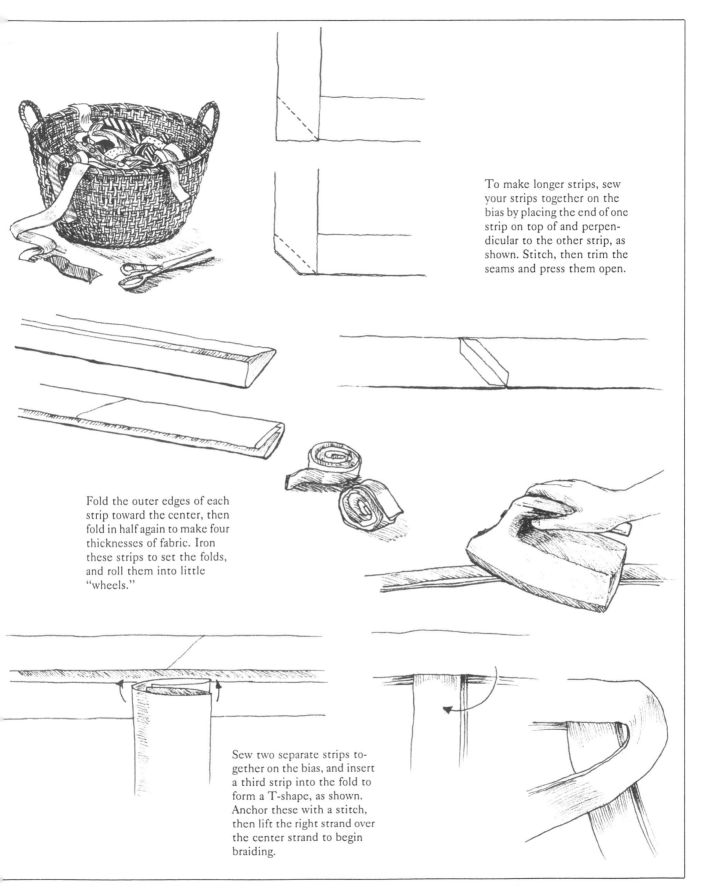

To make longer strips, sew your strips together on the bias by placing the end of one strip on top of and perpendicular to the other strip, as shown. Stitch, then trim the seams and press them open.

Fold the outer edges of each strip toward the center, then fold in half again to make four thicknesses of fabric. Iron these strips to set the folds, and roll them into little "wheels."

Sew two separate strips together on the bias, and insert a third strip into the fold to form a T-shape, as shown. Anchor these with a stitch, then lift the right strand over the center strand to begin braiding.

be certain.

Step 3: After the resist dries, paint your design with specially formulated silk paints, or use Procion dyes with a thickening agent. Heat set by ironing after 48 hours, then wash out clear resist by soaking the project in water.

Tie-Dye, Resist and Batik Suppliers

Pro Chemical & Dye, Inc., P.O. Box 14, Somerset, MA 02726; (508)676-3838. Call or write for their catalog.

Dharma Trading Company. P.O. Box 150916, San Rafael, CA 94915; (800)542-5227. Call or write for their catalog.

Easy Appliquéing—Working With Fusible Web

Fusible web allows you to fuse two different fabrics together, like an appliqué, without laborious hemming. There are several brands, for example, Wonder Under, by Pellon; Transfuse II, by Stacy; and Fine Fuse, by Solar-Kist. Fusible web is great for decorating sweatshirts, T-shirts, pillows, table accessories, and lampshades. Although you still need to do a little sewing, if you've ever appliquéd before, it will seem like nothing. You can also use fusible web as a backing for fabric cutouts used to decorate baskets, in which case you glue, rather than iron it in place.

Step 1: Follow manufacturer's directions to iron fusible web onto your fabric.

Step 2: Either cut out one of the preexisting motifs or patterns from the cloth, or draw your own design on the paper backing of the fusible web. If you have a pattern from a craft magazine, or one you've drawn yourself, you can transfer it to the paper backing using a dressmaker's carbon. Cut out your motif.

Step 3: Remove the protective paper backing, place the fabric motif on your sweatshirt or other item to be decorated, then iron it to fuse.

Step 4: To fully secure the decoration, outline it with dimensional fabric paints. You can also use these paints to highlight parts of the design in coordinated colors. Or stitch around all the edges using invisible nylon thread, a machine zigzag, or an embroidery stitch.

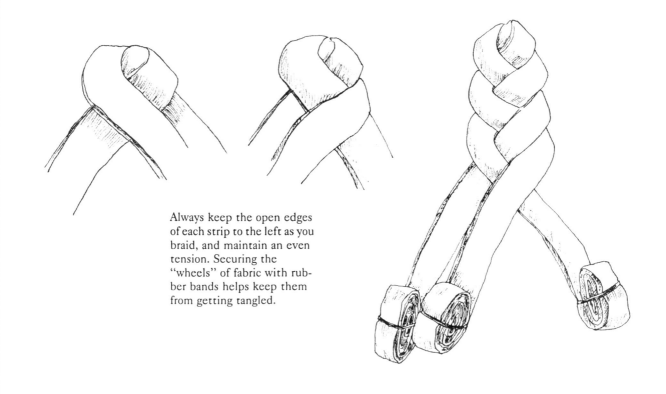

Always keep the open edges of each strip to the left as you braid, and maintain an even tension. Securing the "wheels" of fabric with rubber bands helps keep them from getting tangled.

Braiding a Rag Rug

It doesn't matter if these rugs are placed in front of the fireplace, covering a hardwood floor, or inside the front door—they provide welcome warmth. Rag rugs are a great way to utilize old fabric that's too worn or unattractive to be used in a·quilt. Or you can buy fabric in complementary colors for a more designer look. I've even made rugs out of old ties I purchased at a secondhand store.

You'll need heavy to medium weight fabric (wool or cotton, avoid synthetics), tailor's chalk, a yard stick, sharp scissors, an iron, a sewing machine (though you can sew by hand, if necessary), a large needle, and heavy thread. In selecting your fabrics, choose colors that look good together. Try to find material that's about the same weight.

Step 1: Mark 4-inch wide strips of fabric with tailor's chalk, using the yard stick as a guide. Cut the strips out following the grain of the fabric. (I often just begin the strip with scissors, then tear them the rest of the way by hand.) Using ties saves a lot of time, because you can skip Steps 1 and 2. Machine or hand stitch the strips together on the bias by placing the end of one strip on top of and perpendicular to another, as illustrated on page 63. Trim the seams to ¼ inch; press open. Make a lot of these—it always takes more than you think. As an example, to make the small rug pictured on page 51, I made strips from three dresses, four shirts, two pillowcases, several ties, a denim jumpsuit, and one nightgown.

Step 2: Fold the outer edges of each strip toward the center, so the edges meet. Then fold the strip again so the folded edges meet, creating four thicknesses of fabric. Steam press to set the folds; roll each folded strip around itself to form a wheel.

Step 3: Sew two separate strips together as you did above: place one strip on top of and perpendicular to the other, then stitch on the bias. Lay the joined strips flat; place the end of a third strip between the fold of the first two to make a T-shape. Secure these with a few hand stitches, if desired. As you braid, always keep the open edges of each strip to the left.

Step 4: Begin braiding by lifting the right strand over the center strand. Then lift the left strand over the new center strand. Continue like this, keeping an even tension, but without stretching the braid. Stitch new strips to the working strips as necessary, always on the bias, and continue braiding until your rug reaches the desired dimensions.

Step 5: Sew the braids together using heavy thread and a large needle. Working from the bottom, insert the needle into a space on the rug with an upward stroke, then pick up the loop on the braid with a downward stroke. Sewing it this way interlocks the braid instead of just stitching it side by side. Your next upstroke picks up the adjacent strand of the adjacent braid.

Braiding Place Mats

These are made like the rugs, only using lighter weight fabrics. Coasters can be made using this method, as well. The following information relates the slight differences between the techniques; refer to Rag Rugs for complete instructions.

Step 1: Use at least three different fabrics—calicoes or Liberty prints work well. Cut strips of fabric 1½ inches wide; then sew the ends together on the bias as described for rag rugs. Iron each side under, then fold in half, so you're left with a ½-inch wide strip.

Step 2: Pin three of these long strips to your ironing board, and begin braiding. As the braid lengthens, curl it around itself to form a circle; hold it in place with straight pins.

Step 3: When your mat reaches the size you want, iron it flat, removing the straight pins as you go. Stitch the braid in place as described for rugs.

Step 4: If you want to make a backing for the place mat, cut a piece of fusible web to fit within the circle and iron it onto the back. Then cut a piece of fabric slightly larger than the circle (¾ to 1 inch wider all around). Iron under the edges, then peel the paper off the fusible web and place this fabric circle on top. Iron it to fuse; stitch the edges with invisible nylon thread.

FIVE

GIFTS FROM THE KITCHEN

Sometimes you want to give a gift, but you don't want the person to feel obligated or put on the spot. Homemade goodies can be the perfect way to show you care without making a big deal out of it. Cookies, cakes and pies are the old standbys, but with so many people watching their weight these days, not to mention their cholesterol and sugar intake, giving gifts of sweets is not as fashionable as it once was. Nevertheless, with a little creativity and imagination, you can come up with thoughtful—and delicious—gifts sure to please even the most diet-conscious individuals.

Like what, you ask? Try herb-flavored vinegars, jars of your special sauces, chutney, herb or whole wheat bread, even just a basket of fresh produce. Or what about having a dinner party for friends? Though not traditionally considered a "gift," this can be a wonderful statement of affection, especially considering that time seems to be our most precious commodity nowadays.

Of course there are a lot of people who love sweets, and though they seldom if ever get around to baking, they'll eat the most sinfully rich desserts in restaurants. Though they may moan about calories, these people would love traditional gifts like a plate of brownies for an office birthday party, or an assortment of cookies during the holidays. Giving dessert-type gifts in a group or party situation offers a way for people to partake or not, as they choose.

To save time, when you do get around to baking bread, or cooking up some special sauces, double the recipe and freeze the extra for some later gift-giving occasion. It's a great feeling to know there are loaves of banana, zucchini and carrot bread in the freezer, and all you have to do is tie on a festive ribbon and go! Handmade labels give food gifts an extra personal touch; you'll find instructions for making them in Chapter Seven.

Another idea is just to give recipes, which people can use or not, at their own discretion. A recipe printed neatly on a card, and tied with ribbon to a geranium, for instance, would be appropriate for a housewarming gift. For someone special who's getting married or moving into his or her first apartment, a personalized cookbook of your favorite, time-tested recipes might make a great present. For more details, read on.

IDEAS

The following list includes health-conscious food ideas as well as suggestions for the more self-indulgent on your list. You probably know who's who, but if there's any doubt, observe his or her eating habits!

Recipes: Good cooks love to share. When you give an unusual gift of food, something that regularly gets rave reviews, pass along the recipe as well. If possible, find out how the cook you intend to share with catalogs her recipes, and present it in that format. Type or write up the recipe so it will fit on a standard recipe card (there are two sizes) or a sheet of paper. Then photocopy several copies, because favorite recipes tend to be requested often.

Personalized Cookbook: This is a great gift to give yourself, as well as young people who've just moved away from home or gotten married. Start with a loose-leaf notebook and clear plastic sheet dividers, available at office supply stores; you may want to decorate the notebook by covering it with cloth, decoupage (see Chapter Six) or with a stamping technique (refer to Chapter Four for How-To's).

Now, just photocopy your favorite recipes and slip them between the sheet dividers. Recipes printed on only one side can be stapled or glued to the black construction paper insert; for recipes printed on both sides of a page, remove the insert and staple them directly to the clear plastic. Separate categories with tab dividers marked as Entrees, Soups, Breads and Desserts.

Jar of Spiced Nuts: Easy and quick to make, and oh-so-delicious to eat, spiced nuts make good gifts for hostesses, neighbors and friends. Start with a pound of nuts—pecans, almonds and peanuts are prime candidates for the spice treatment, but try others as well. Beat one egg white, add a cup of sugar, and a heaping teaspoon of cinnamon. (Also try adding ½ teaspoon of allspice, ¼ teaspoon each of nutmeg and ginger—even a pinch of coriander.) Roll the nuts in this mixture, then spread them out on a cookie sheet or cake pan, and bake for an hour in a 200 degree oven. Be sure to turn the nuts every fifteen minutes to prevent them from sticking.

Once cool, put the spiced nuts in a decorative jar or tin. Recycle empty glass jars by painting their lids or attaching a square of cloth with elastic ribbon. You could also paint designs on the glass jar itself.

Pepitas: Street vendors all over Mexico sell pepitas—fried pumpkin seeds—as snacks. They're easy and inexpensive to make—all you need are fresh pumpkin seeds. Adored by people with a taste for the unusual as well as those who subscribe to the "waste not, want not" school, pepitas surprise even the skeptical with their nutty flavor. When you carve your jack o'lantern at Halloween, instead of throwing away the seeds, separate them from the pulp and rinse them, then lay them on paper towels to dry. Once dry, fry them in olive oil until golden brown, sprinkle with salt, and drain on paper towels. Once cool, pack them in glass jars or small decorative tins.

Trail Mix: This treat for the health-conscious is a cinch to make. The simplest way is to combine raisins and peanuts, but truly health-conscious folks will spurn it unless you use organically grown ingredients. You can jazz it up by adding sunflower seeds, walnuts and dried fruits like apricots, apples, dates and coconut. Put everything in a recycled jar which you've decorated yourself.

Fruit Leather: Another healthful treat, though it does contain some sugar, is apricot or peach leather. Easy to make and fun to eat, fruit leather strips look beautiful when presented in a clear glass jar. To make them, simply pour a cup of boiling water over a pound of dried apricots or dried peaches, and let them soak for 12 hours. (If you use tenderized fruit omit this step.) Grind the fruit in a food processor or blender, then roll it out on a board covered with powdered sugar. Keep rolling until it's about $1/16$ of an inch thick,

adding more powdered sugar as necessary. Cut the roll into strips, roll them up loosely and place in an airtight tin or jar. Adding a little grated lemon rind to the blender or processor before you roll out the fruit lends a nice tang.

Vegetable Basket: This variation on the fruit basket can be a good gift to give neighbors and friends if you have a large garden. Gather tomatoes, zucchini, peppers, broccoli and any other produce that's ripe and assemble them in a willow basket. (You could line the basket with a pretty cloth, but it's not necessary.) Bestow these harvest baskets on people who like homegrown vegetables.

Flavored Vinegars: Great gifts for dieters and gourmets, vinegars seasoned with fresh herbs, chilis,

Jars of homemade pickles, preserves, spiced nuts and vinegars that were "put by" in the summertime can be given as gifts at Christmas.

ginger or garlic taste sensational and are easy to make. Use distilled white, apple cider or wine vinegar, and choose from a vast variety of flavoring ingredients. In an enamel or stainless steel pan, heat three gallons of vinegar to just below boiling, then add sprigs of fresh tarragon, thyme, rosemary, savory, chervil, peppercorns, or garlic — or use your own favorite combination of herbs. Remove the garlic after 24 hours. (It is very important to remove the garlic, and to allow no more than 3 tablespoons of fresh herbs per quart of vinegar, to prevent botulism.) Let the rest of the mixture steep for two to four weeks before straining it and pouring it into sterilized glass bottles. Cork the bottles tightly or use noncorrodible tops. You can add homemade labels and tie a cloth ribbon around the neck for an extra touch.

Homemade Preserves: Jars of jelly, with their beautiful, jewel-like colors, are food gifts that last longer than most. Some recipes for jams, jellies, preserves, marmalades and apple butters take a little time to make, but think how many gifts you'll have when you're done! If you've never canned or "put food by," you may feel intimidated by the process, but if you can follow directions, it's really not complicated. Some recipes are easier than others, and require less preparation; if you use jars with a two-piece metal screw down lid, for instance, there's no need to use paraffin. Comprehensive cookbooks such as *The Joy of Cooking* and *The Fanny Farmer Cookbook* contain a variety of recipes as well as detailed instructions. See the How-To section of this chapter for a quick jalapeño jelly. Make jellies in the summer when produce is cheap and plentiful, then give the jars at Christmastime. Handmade labels add cheer!

Jars of Pickles: Like preserves, pickles are made in summer to be enjoyed on dreary winter days — though of course you don't have to wait that long. They range from dill and sweet pickled cucumbers to watermelon pickles and tomato chutney, from corn relish to brandied pears. They're easy, if somewhat time consuming to make, but they keep on giving once delivered. Complete instructions and a variety of recipes can be found in comprehensive cookbooks such as *The Joy of Cooking*. Top jars with a square of colorful cloth, held in place by a rubber band or elastic ribbon; homemade labels or gift tags are another nice touch.

Special Sauces: Here's an unusual idea that makes a good gift for people who love food but are too busy to cook. Make up a big batch of your favorite spaghetti, pesto or barbeque sauce (see the How-To section for my favorites), then pour the sauce into freezer containers or Tupperware. Label the containers clearly, then freeze. When you're ready to give them, use ribbon to tie on a copy of the recipe, and hand deliver the container to your friend's freezer. You could also use glass jars to be kept in the refrigerator, but the recipient would need to use the sauce within a week or two, unless you used a canning technique to package it.

Chutneys: These spicy relishes are a staple of Indian cuisine and make an exotic gift for anyone with a taste for the unusual. They may contain tomatoes and apples, or peaches, papaya and apricot with an abundance of onions, garlic, ginger, cayenne, pepper and vinegar. Check out an Indian cookbook or *The Joy of Cooking* for recipes. Chutneys complement lentil and other bean dishes, so they're a great gift for vegetarians.

Quick Breads: Easy and inexpensive to make, usually more like cake than bread, quick breads are universally appreciated. Bake up batches of honey, oatmeal, zucchini, banana, carrot, pumpkin, cranberry, apricot or prune bread and freeze them ahead for the holidays, or unexpected gift-giving occasions. Wrapped in aluminum foil or clear plastic wrap and tied with ribbon and a bow, a dessert bread makes a sweet present. See the How-To section for a few of my favorite recipes.

Yeast Breads: Since you must wait for the dough to rise, these breads take a little longer to make, but correspondingly, people tend to be even more impressed. "You made this?" they ask. "Wow, that's a lot of work!" Kneading is an extra step, but that part can be fun (especially if you need a little exercise or want to release frustration), and letting it rise is really not that big a deal, because meanwhile you can read, talk on the phone, do housework, wash your hair, or just relax. If you're strapped for time, there are some good "rapid rise" recipes for yeast breads that cut preparation time in half. Some batter bread recipes even eliminate the kneading. Check your cookbook (*Betty Crocker's Cookbook* has several excellent recipes), and see the How-To section for an example.

As with quick breads, yeast breads can be baked ahead and frozen for later. They can be baked with herbs, garlic, poppy seeds, cheese and eggs and can be formed into interesting shapes for baking—I've seen turtles, fish and even a basket woven of strips of dough then filled with "fruit" made out of bread. More useful as a centerpiece than to eat, elaborate presentations like these are nevertheless very impressive. They should be shellacked to help preserve them.

A Cake: This is a time-honored way to welcome new neighbors. Packaged cakes are easy and quick, but if you have time, a made from scatch cake is a nice gesture. An apple cake, easy sour cream cake, or apricot chocolate chip torte (see the How-To section for recipes) sends a delicious message to newcomers. You can also provide the recipe, neatly lettered or typed on a card.

Coffee Cakes and Cinnamon Rolls: For a coffee klatch or brunch, you can't beat the flavor—and aroma!—of baked goods fresh from the oven. Coffee cake recipes are usually quick (no yeast), and incorporate everything from chocolate to pineapple; cinnamon rolls usually need to rise, but there are some

Although not usually thought of as "food," a gourmet herbal wreath can be hung in the kitchen and its ingredients used to flavor all kinds of dishes. Refer to Chapter Three for how-to make wreaths. Always remember to use U-shaped pins or floral picks rather than a glue gun on decorations that might be consumed.

shortcuts. See the How-To section for a quick cinnamon roll recipe.

Cheesecake: Whether topped with cherries or swirled with chocolate, who can resist the velvety richness of a deli cheesecake? Bake one for someone's birthday, precut it, and slip freezer paper between the pieces so it can be popped in the freezer and eaten piece by piece over a period of time. A cheesecake provides birthday greetings to last all year—or at least a few weeks, depending on the person's level of obsession! See the How-To section for a luscious recipe.

Cookies: A tin or plate of assorted cookies is a standard holiday gift that appeals to anyone with a sweet tooth. They also make great presents for busy hostesses, who will thank you for saving them time. To get the requisite variety of colors, shapes and flavors, make up batches of different kinds of cookies and freeze them in the months before Christmas. That way you'll be way ahead of the game. In addition to the standard Christmas sugar cookies and rum balls, try molasses cookies, almond meringue cookies, date bars and Mexican wedding cookies. (Recipes are provided in the How-To section.) You may also want to include some homemade candy. As an alternative to the old standby plate or tin, try presenting cookies in a basket lined with colorful tissue paper; wrap ribbon around the handle and tie on a handmade gift tag.

Candy: Visions of sugar plums—and fudge, pralines, taffy, toffee, caramel corn, peanut brittle, sugared nuts . . . If you've never made candy before, you may be intimidated by the terminology—soft ball, hard ball, soft crack—but candy making really isn't difficult. A candy thermometer is crucial for most recipes, but even kids can make candy if they can follow a recipe. And sugared nuts are foolproof, as long as you remember to stir them every 15 minutes. (For a recipe, see Jar of Spiced Nuts, earlier in this section.) Give sweets to the sweet!

Gourmet Wreath: An aromatic wreath made from herbs such as oregano, thyme, dill, basil, garlic, sage and red peppers would make a wonderful gift for someone who cooks. Refer to Chapter Three for instructions on wreath making.

Festive Meal Ideas

Dinner Party: We don't usually think of dinner parties as gifts, but entertaining can be seen as a generalized gift to a group of friends. You take the time to plan an interesting menu, invite people, make your house comfortable and inviting, and cook a wonderful meal. The classic dinner party is for six to eight people; by setting up several tables you may be able to accommodate more, but I prefer the intimacy of a smaller gathering. The meal includes a good cut of meat, say, a standing rib roast, chicken breasts, or a delicately flavored fish, such as whitefish, trout or salmon, served with baked potatoes, steamed vegetables and bread. Italian foods like lasagne or gnochi are also popular. I like to make an elegant casserole of stuffed shells and serve it with zucchini sauted in wine, as well as salad and garlic bread. See the How-To section for recipes.

Southern-style Barbeque: Show a group of friends some Southern hospitality with a meal of barbequed ribs, red beans and rice, corn bread, tossed salad, vanilla ice cream and pecan pie. Serve with beer or iced tea. Barbequed chicken could be substituted for ribs, or for that matter, grill hamburgers and hot dogs instead. Served on the deck or patio, this makes a great summer cookout. See the How-To section for recipes.

Mexican Fiesta: Mexican food is flavorful yet inexpensive, and easy to fix. It has a naturally festive quality. Serve fresh salsa with chips as an appetizer, with a main dish of burritos or tacos, or try my Hot Stuff Calzone, which always draws rave reviews, served with red cabbage salad and sugar cookies. (See the How-To section for recipes.) You may have noticed that this menu is not "purist." Mexicans use red cabbage more as a garnish, making salads of green cabbage, and the calzone is traditionally an Italian dish, but it's reinterpreted here with various types of chili peppers. For that matter, you never see burritos in Mexico—they're pure Tex-Mex.

Vegetarian Feast: If you have friends who are vegetarians—or maybe you're one yourself—you know what a hard time non-vegetarians have cooking without meat. Serving a meat-free meal is a great way to let people know you respect their choice, and it's a valuable experience for meat eaters, as well. There are some wonderful vegetarian cookbooks. Molly Katz's cookbooks (*Still Life with Menu*, *The Enchanted Broccoli Forest*, and the original, *Moosewood Cookbook*) are especially good. These foods are so flavorful that

carnivores don't know what they're missing, and in the process of preparing them, you may find yourself turned on to a whole new style of cuisine.

The Lunch Bunch: Now that many of us work full time outside the home, serving lunch is a luxury few can afford. Oh sure, we meet for lunch at a restaurant, but the idea of homecooking is just a joke. We're too busy. And that's precisely why this idea works— you take the time to create a delicious noonday meal for your friends. Plan it for some Saturday, or even a weekday if you can arrange your schedule. (If your workplace allows flex time, there's no problem; you could even take a half day vacation.) The menu can be simple: pesto and rotini, or curried tuna salad served on toasted bagels or pita bread, fruit salad and cookies. This can be a fun way to get together to compare notes, network and gossip.

RECIPE HOW-TO'S
Here are some of my favorite recipes for gift-giving, including recipes from the party menus discussed in the Ideas section. You probably have your own favorite recipes, but if you want additional ideas, visit your public library and browse through the cookbook section.

QUICK BREADS
Quick breads are made from batter, as cakes are. You don't have to knead them or wait for them to rise. They use baking powder, soda, or both as a leavening agent, and are usually moist and rich. Most of my favorite recipes contain nuts. To increase your yields, use several small pans and shorten the baking time.

Exotic Banana Bread
This recipe makes a rich, delicious loaf with a flavor that's much more complex than the average banana bread.

2 cups flour	1½ cups mashed bananas
½ cup oatmeal (uncooked)	1 tablespoon grated orange rind
1 teaspoon baking soda	¼ cup buttermilk
½ teaspoon salt	1 teaspoon vanilla
1 cup sugar	1 cup shredded coconut
½ cup margarine	¾ cup chopped nuts
2 eggs	

1. Preheat oven to 350 degrees. Mix together flour, oats, soda and salt. Set aside.
2. Cream sugar and margarine; add eggs, bananas and orange rind.
3. Combine buttermilk and vanilla.
4. Alternately add the dry ingredients and buttermilk to the butter and sugar mix, beginning and ending with the dry ingredients. Blend well.
5. Stir in coconut and nuts.
6. Pour into a greased and floured 9×5-inch pan. Bake in a 350 degree oven for 70 minutes.
7. Cool for 10 minutes in the pan. Remove the bread from the pan and finish cooling on rack.

Yield: One loaf

1. Preheat oven to 350 degrees. Blend butter, sugar, eggs and vanilla until smooth and creamy.
2. Add remaining ingredients slowly, stirring well to mix.
3. Grease and flour two 8×4-inch loaf pans; divide the batter evenly between them.
4. Bake for an hour at 350 degrees; allow the bread to cool for at least 10 minutes before removing it from the pan.

Yield: Two loaves

Nutty Zucchini Bread

In summertime, avid gardeners share bumper crops of vegetables with friends, neighbors and coworkers. If you want to dress up a gift of zucchini, try this recipe for one of the easiest, most delicious quick breads I've ever tasted. Serve it at a party and watch it disappear—within moments.

1 cup butter or margarine, softened (2 sticks)

2 cups sugar

3 eggs, beaten

2 teaspoons vanilla

2 cups unbleached flour

½ cup oatmeal (uncooked)

½ teaspoon baking powder

2 teaspoons soda

1 teaspoon salt

3 teaspoons cinnamon

1½ teaspoons allspice

3 cups zucchini, grated (about 3 medium zucchini)

1½ cups walnuts, chopped

1 cup raisins

Combine yeast breads and quick breads in a basket to give as a tasteful hostess or housewarming gift.

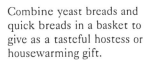

Irish Soda Bread

This bread is sweet and crumbly, and great for breakfast, brunch or snacks. Wrapped in aluminum foil and tied with a festive ribbon, the distinctive round loaves make great gifts.

4 cups sifted flour	1 cup raisins
1 teaspoon salt	1 tablespoon caraway
1 teaspoon baking soda	seeds
1 cup sugar	1½ cups buttermilk
¾ cup butter	

1. Sift the dry ingredients together.
2. Add butter, cut fine with a pastry blender or fork.
3. Add raisins and caraway; gradually add buttermilk.
4. Turn the dough onto a floured board and work it for 1 minute. Add a little more flour if necessary to manage the dough, but it should remain somewhat sticky.
5. Cut the dough in half; form it into two balls.
6. Put the dough on a greased baking sheet and make a bold impression of a cross in the top. (This not only has the practical effect of preventing the bread from cracking as it bakes, but also acts as a kind of invocation.)
7. Brush the top with buttermilk, then bake the bread in a preheated 350 degree oven for 45 to 50 minutes, or until golden brown.

Yield: Two loaves

YEAST BREADS

Though they take a little longer to prepare, yeast breads are "the staff of life" and people take them seriously. Many cooks find the kneading process theraputic, and you can't beat the aroma of freshly baked bread just out of the oven. Bake an extra loaf or two as a gift for the family.

Herb Nut Bread

This flavorful bread is great for the health nuts on your list—and anyone who appreciates good home-made bread.

3 cups warm water	3 tablespoons dill weed
½ to ¾ cup honey	3 tablespoons parsley
3 heaping tablespoons active dry yeast	3 tablespoons poppy seed
	3 tablespoons onion
1 teaspoon salt	3 cloves garlic

4½ cups unbleached flour	¾ cup olive oil
4½ cups whole wheat flour	1 cup oats
	1 cup sunflower seeds
1 egg	½ cup sesame seeds

1. Mix the honey and warm water together; add the yeast. (Active dry yeast works best in water that's between 105 and 115 degrees.) Set the mixture aside.
2. Sauté the onion and garlic in butter. Add salt, dill, parsley and poppy seed to the sauté pan, then mix these into the yeast water.
3. Add 3 to 5 cups of flour, egg, oil, oats, sunflower seeds and sesame seeds. Mix well.
4. Add the remaining flour; turn the dough onto a floured board and knead until the dough is smooth and elastic (5 to 10 minutes), adding more flour if necessary to manage the dough.
5. Shape the dough into a large ball, place it in a greased bowl, then cover the bowl and let the dough rise about an hour or until doubled in size.
6. When the dough is doubled, punch it down; let it rise again for about 30 minutes or until almost doubled in bulk.
7. Shape the dough into loaves; place it in oiled pans, cover and let it rise 15 minutes.
8. Oil tops of loaves and bake them about 30 minutes at 350 degrees.

Yield: Two loaves

Cool-Rise White Bread

This unusual recipe uses extra hot water and undis-solved yeast. It has an abbreviated rising period, and the dough can be held in the refrigerator for 2 to 12 hours before baking. This is great for when you want to serve fresh bread at a dinner party—just prepare the dough the day before, then pop it in the oven an hour before the meal.

7¾ to 8¾ cups unsifted flour	3 packages active dry yeast
3 tablespoons sugar	⅓ cup softened margarine
4½ teaspoons salt	2¾ cups water (120 to 130 degrees)

1. Thoroughly mix 3 cups flour, sugar, salt and *undis-solved* yeast. Add margarine.

2. Gradually add hot water to the dry ingredients and, with an electric mixer, beat 2 minutes on medium speed.
3. Add ½ cup flour; beat on high speed for 2 minutes.
4. Stir in enough additional flour to make a stiff dough. Turn the dough onto a floured board; knead until it is smooth and elastic (about 10 to 12 minutes).
5. Cover the dough with plastic wrap, then a towel. Let the dough rise 20 minutes.
6. Divide the dough in half, then roll it out into two 14×9-inch rectangles. Shape the dough into loaves; then place them in greased pans. Brush with vegetable oil.
7. Cover the loaves loosely and refrigerate for 2 to 12 hours.
8. When ready to bake the loaves, preheat the oven to 400 degrees. Uncover the dough and let it stand at room temperature for at least 10 minutes. Puncture any bubbles that may have formed.
9. Bake at 400 degrees for 35 to 40 minutes.

Yield: Two loaves

90-Minute Cinnamon Rolls

Great for a coffee klatch or brunch, or try putting these sweet rolls in a napkin-lined basket and delivering to a friend or neighbor. I found this recipe on the back of a Fleischmann's Yeast package fifteen years ago and have loved it ever since. (It is reprinted here courtesy of Fleischmann's.)

1 package Fleischmann's Rapid Rise Yeast	1 tablespoon melted butter
½ cup warm water (105 to 115 degrees)	⅓ cup sugar
3 tablespoons sugar	1 teaspoon cinnamon
½ teaspoon salt	½ teaspoon nutmeg
2 tablespoons softened butter	½ teaspoon cloves
1 egg	⅓ cup dark seedless raisins
2 to 2½ cups unsifted flour	½ cup powdered sugar
	1 tablespoon warm water

1. Have all the ingredients at room temperature. Dissolve the yeast in warm water.
2. Beat in 3 tablespoons sugar, 2 tablespoons butter, egg, and 1 cup flour.

3. Stir in enough additional flour to make a soft dough.
4. Turn the dough out onto a floured board; knead it about 2 minutes, or until it is smooth.
5. Roll the dough out to an 18×9-inch rectangle. Brush with melted butter.
6. Mix together ⅓ cup sugar, cinnamon, nutmeg, cloves and raisins. Sprinkle the mixture on top of the buttered dough.
7. Roll the dough up as if for a jelly roll; seal the sides firmly.
8. Cut the roll into twelve equal pieces; arrange them cut side down on a greased 8-inch round pan.
9. Pour boiling water into a large baking pan and place it on the center rack of a cold oven. Set the rolls on a wire rack over the pan of water. Cover the rolls.
10. Let the rolls rise 30 minutes. Then uncover them, remove the pan of water and the rack.
11. Turn the oven on to 375 degrees and bake the rolls 30 to 35 minutes.
12. Mix powdered sugar with a tablespoon of water to make a glaze. While rolls are still warm, dribble glaze on top.

Yield: Twelve rolls

COOKIES

When putting together an assortment of cookies, go for a variety of colors, shapes and tastes. Bar cookies are easiest, because all you do is press them into the pan then cut them, while a cookie press can speed up the "drop" cookie process. Kids love to help, so baking cookies can be a fun project for everybody to help with. Some of my favorite recipes are included here.

Delicious Date Bars

These are old staples of my Christmas cookie collection. They're easy to make, very popular with cookie consumers, and they help keep other cookies moist.

3 cups (1 pound) dates, chopped	¾ cup butter or margarine, softened
¼ cup honey	1 cup brown sugar, packed
1½ cups water	1 teaspoon cinnamon
1 cup walnuts	

Make someone happy with a gift of food. Pictured clockwise from the top: bran and date bars, zucchini bread and herb nut bread, a jar of spiced nuts, molasses cookies and Mexican wedding cookies, sugar cookies and Irish soda bread.

1¾ cups flour	1½ cups oatmeal,
1 teaspoon salt	uncooked
½ teaspoon soda	

1. To make the filling, combine the chopped dates, honey and water in a medium saucepan and cook over low heat for 10 minutes, or until the mixture thickens. Remove the mixture from the heat; add the walnuts. Allow the mixture to cool. (Put the pan in the refrigerator for faster results.)
2. Preheat the oven to 400 degrees. Cream the butter and sugar; mix in the remaining ingredients. Spread half of this mixture in the bottom of a greased 13 × 9-inch pan.
3. Spread the filling over this; top with the remaining mixture. Pat the dough down lightly.
4. Bake for 25 to 30 minutes. Cut the cookies into bars while still warm.

Yield: Three dozen 2 × 1½-inch bars

Myra's Raspberry Bars

Myra Griffin's Dionysus restaurant has been a fixture in Cincinnati since 1977. The atmosphere is cozy, and the menu features a variety of vegetarian dishes. This is one of their most popular desserts. If you have a food processor, you can whip these up in nothing flat; even made the old fashioned way, with a pastry blender, they take less than 15 minutes to prepare.

3 cups white flour	1 egg
1 cup white sugar	¾ to 1 cup raspberry jam
1½ cups sliced whole	(I use one of the all
almonds	fruit, no sugar added
1 cup butter, cold	jams.)
1 cup mini-chocolate	
chips	

1. Preheat the oven to 350 degrees.
2. Grind the flour and almonds to a fine paste. (If you don't have a food processor, grind the nuts in the blender or a grinder before mixing with the flour.)
3. Add chunks of butter; blend the mixture until it is mealy.
4. Add the egg and sugar.
5. Press half of this mixture into the bottom of a greased 9 × 13-inch pan.

6. Spread raspberry jam on top of the mixture; sprinkle chocolate chips on top of the jam.
7. Spread the rest of the almond mixture on top and pat down lightly.
8. Bake for 35 minutes or until golden brown. Cut into bars while warm.

Yield: Three dozen 3 × 1½-inch bars

Chewy Bran Bars

These bar cookies are quick, easy, delicious and full of fiber, too!

2 tablespoons butter	1 teaspoon vanilla
¼ cup peanut butter	⅛ teaspoon salt
¼ cup brown sugar	½ cup raisins, prunes or
½ cup honey	dates
1½ cups chopped nuts	2 cups whole bran cereal
2 teaspoons cinnamon	

1. Heat the butter, peanut butter, brown sugar and honey in a large saucepan until the mixture just begins to boil. Remove the pan from the heat.
2. Stir in chopped nuts, cinnamon, vanilla and salt.
3. Add cereal and raisins, prunes or dates. Stir until they are well coated.
4. With a spatula, press the mixture into a well greased 8 or 9-inch square pan to form an even layer.
5. Let the mixture cool 5 minutes, then cut it into bars. Allow the bars to cool more before serving.

Yield: Twelve to sixteen cookies

Old-Fashioned Sugar Cookies

This is a wonderful old recipe handed down from my friend Mike Heldman's great-grandmother Huttenbauer. Written on notebook paper in his grandmother's hand, the recipe mainly lists ingredients. But he remembers watching his grandmother make these shortbread treats, and helped me fill in the instructions.

1 cup butter (two sticks)	1 teaspoon baking powder
1¾ cups sugar, sifted	Topping:
3 eggs, well beaten	Cinnamon
1 teaspoon vanilla	Granulated sugar
4 cups flour	

1. Beat butter and sugar in a large bowl until they are fluffy.
2. Add eggs and vanilla and continue beating as you gradually add the dry ingredients.
3. Refrigerate the dough several hours or overnight.
4. Preheat the oven to 370 degrees. Roll out ⅓ of the dough at a time on a lightly floured surface, to about a ⅜-inch thickness. The dough should be very thin.
5. Cut the dough into rectangles about 1½ × 4 inches; then place them on greased cookie sheets. Run the tines of a fork down the center of each cookie to make indentations, then sprinkle them with cinnamon and sugar.
6. Bake the cookies for 10 minutes or until they are just lightly brown; cool them on a rack.

Yield: Four dozen cookies

Spicy Molasses Cookies

These easy-to-make cookies are a wonderful addition to a plate of Christmas cookies. The recipe comes from Martha Vieth Petry, who got it from her mother.

¾ cup butter or margarine	2 teaspoons soda
1 cup brown sugar	½ teaspoon salt
1 egg	1 teaspoon ginger
¼ cup molasses	1 teaspoon cinnamon
2½ cups flour	1 teaspoon cloves

1. Blend the butter, sugar, egg and molasses until they are smooth and creamy.
2. Sift in the dry ingredients and stir until they are blended.
3. Chill the dough for 2 hours. (If you have time, this makes the dough easier to manage, but I sometimes omit this step—or stick the bowl in the freezer for 10 minutes or so.)
4. Shape the dough into little balls the size of walnuts.
5. Place the cookies on a greased cookie sheet and bake them in a preheated 375 degree oven for about 12 minutes.

Yield: About three dozen cookies

Mexican Wedding Cookies

These cookies are great in Christmas assortments because they look like snowballs. (Not to mention the fact that they're delicious.) This recipe comes from Margaret Harold, a high school Spanish teacher who served them at the annual Spanish Club banquet.

½ cup powered sugar	2¼ cups flour
1 cup butter, chopped in small pieces	¼ teaspoon salt
	¾ cup chopped nuts
1 teaspoon vanilla	

1. Mix butter, vanilla and sugar thoroughly.
2. Stir the flour and salt together, and blend them with the butter mixture.
3. Add the nuts and stir.
4. Chill the dough.
5. Preheat the oven to 400 degrees.
6. Roll the dough into 1-inch balls; place them on an ungreased cookie sheet. (These cookies don't spread.)
7. Bake the cookies for 10 to 12 minutes, or until they are set but not brown.
8. While the cookies are still warm, roll them in confectioner's sugar. Cool the cookies then roll them again.

Yield: Four dozen cookies

Nana's Very Special Almond Cookies

Every Christmas we looked forward to my grandmother's special almond cookies, so light they practically melt in your mouth. The almonds are ground fine and act as "flour"; the eggs must be beaten thoroughly, but it's worth it! This is a heavenly cookie.

2 pounds unblanched almonds, ground to powder	2 pounds powdered sugar
	1 vanilla bean (or 4 teaspoons vanilla)
8 egg whites	

1. Preheat oven to 325 degrees.
2. Beat the eggs to a stiff froth. Add the sugar and beat the mixture well. (Nana's recipe says "beat for 15 minutes," but that was before the days of electric mixers.)
3. Set aside half of this mixture to use for icing. Mix

Delicate heirlooms can be
transformed into pillows. All
you need to do is sew a doily
or piece of lace onto a plain
pillow. You can also frame
doilies after stitching them
to a contrasting fabric.

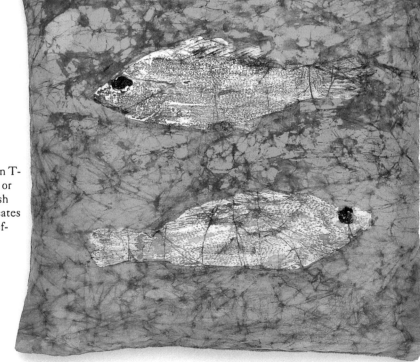

Fish prints can be used on T-
shirts, notepads, pillows or
paper. Batiking over a fish
print, as shown here, creates
a beautiful underwater effect.

Matching napkins and place mats make a great gift for housewarmings, bridal showers, birthdays and holidays. These were
made by carving designs on potato halves that were then
painted and stamped onto the material.

the remainder with the pulverized almonds and vanilla bean (cut fine).

4. Roll out the dough. If it is gooey, add powdered sugar.
5. Cut the dough into strips and spread them with the set aside icing.
6. Bake the cookies for 8 to 10 minutes or just until the strips begin to color.

Yield: Three dozen cookies

German Honey Cakes (Lebkucken)

This recipe for German Honey Cakes was passed down from my grandmother's aunt Frances. The original recipe specified that you should "let the dough sit for two or three days, to ripen," but I've updated that to "overnight in the refrigerator." The recipe makes a slew of cookies, which will keep for up to six months in a tightly sealed tin.

1 pound honey	½ pound blanched
2 cups light brown sugar	almonds
¼ cup water	¼ pound citron
5½ cups unbleached flour	¼ pound candied orange
½ teaspoon baking soda	rind
¼ teaspoon cloves	2 eggs
¼ teaspoon cinnamon	

Transparent Icing for German Honey Cakes

1 cup confectioner's sugar	¼ cup lemon juice
5 teaspoons boiling water	1 teaspoon vanilla

1. Heat honey, brown sugar and water to boiling and simmer for 5 minutes. Remove the mixture from the heat and allow it to cool.
2. Sift together the flour, soda and spices. Once the honey mixture cools, slowly stir in this dry mixture.
3. Add eggs, almonds, citron and orange peel.
4. Work the dough into a loaf, and allow it to age overnight in the refrigerator in a covered crock.
5. The next day, remove the dough from the refrigerator and allow it to reach room temperature. Then work it again, lightly, adding more flour if necessary to prevent sticking.
6. Roll the dough out to ¼-inch thickness, then cut it into 1 × 3-inch pieces.
7. Preheat the oven to 350 degrees. Bake the cookies

on greased sheets for 15 minutes.
8. Combine the ingredients of the transparent icing and mix until it is smooth. Spread this on the cookies while they're still warm.

Yield: About eight dozen cookies

CAKES

"If I knew you were coming, I'd have baked a cake." This homespun saying is a recipe for hospitality. Besides being a birthday standard, cakes are a great way to greet new neighbors. Here are three foolproof recipes for scratch cakes that are an old-fashioned way to say "Welcome!"

Sour Cream Cake

This is the first cake I ever baked successfully from scratch—and it got rave reviews. (I had tried once before this and concluded that mixes were better!) This one is easy and it needs no icing; it's better than any mix. The recipe comes from Gloria Esenwein.

1 cup butter	2 cups flour
2 cups sugar	1 teaspoon baking powder
2 eggs	¼ teaspoon salt
1 cup sour cream	1 cup nuts
½ teaspoon vanilla	1 cup chocolate chips

1. Preheat the oven to 350 degrees. Cream the butter and sugar; beat in the eggs.
2. Add the sour cream and vanilla and mix well.
3. Add the flour, salt and baking powder and mix.
4. Add the nuts and chocolate chips and mix.
5. Bake the batter in a well greased and floured Bundt pan for 1 hour and 20 minutes.

Apple Cake

An excellent "keeper," this unusual cake stays moist for days. Use tart apples—Granny Smiths are good—and bake as either a sheet cake or in layers. This recipe comes from Gladys Dood and Myra Griffin.

1½ cups sugar	2 eggs, beaten
4 cups coarsely chopped	2 teaspoons vanilla
apples	2 cups flour
½ cup cooking oil	2 teaspoons baking soda

1 teaspoon salt	2 cups brown sugar
2 teaspoons cinnamon	½ cup butter
1 cup chopped walnuts	½ cup cream

1. Combine the sugar and apples; let this mixture stand for 3 hours. (If you're strapped for time, this time can be shortened—or eliminated altogether. Just chop the apples into smaller pieces.)
2. Add the oil, eggs and 1 teaspoon of vanilla.
3. Sift the flour, soda, salt and cinnamon together.
4. Stir these dry ingredients into the apple mixture; add the walnuts.
5. Pour the batter into a greased and floured 9 × 13-inch pan. To make a layer cake, use two 9-inch layer pans. Grease the pans, then place baking paper or waxed paper in the bottoms of the pans, and grease and flour the paper. This will prevent the apples from sticking.
6. Bake at 350 degrees for 40 minutes.
7. To make the topping, combine brown sugar, butter and cream in a saucepan.
8. Mix these ingredients well, bringing them to a boil, then, stirring constantly, cook them for 2 minutes, or until the mixture reaches 238 degrees on a candy thermometer.
9. Remove the mixture from the heat; add a teaspoon of vanilla. Beat the ingredients until they are creamy, then spread this icing on the warm sheet cake. For layer cakes, make sure the cake is cool, then pour half the icing on one layer before adding the top. Pour the icing on—it will make "icicles" down the sides.

Apricot Chocolate Chip Torte

Here's another wonderful treat from Myra Griffin, owner of Myra's Dionysus Restaurant in Cincinnati.

2 cups white flour	2 egg yolks
1 cup brown sugar	1 cup cold butter, cut into
1 cup oatmeal	small pieces
2 tablespoons unsweetened cocoa	1½ cups walnuts
	1 cup chocolate chips
2 teaspoons vanilla	1 cup apricot jam

1. Preheat the oven to 350 degrees. Mix the flour,

Nobody bothers to make scratch cakes anymore, but that makes them even better gifts! Loaded with chocolate chips and baked in a Bundt pan, this Sour Cream Cake is one of the best I've ever tasted. It's proved to be a big hit at parties.

sugar, oatmeal, cocoa, vanilla and egg yolks together until mealy.

2. Cut in the butter and walnuts, then mix until mealy.

3. Cut in the chocolate chips.

4. Spread half of this mixture on the bottom of a 10-inch spring form pan.

5. Spread apricot jam over the top of the mixture. Cover it with the rest of the flour mixture. Pat it down in the pan.

6. If using a 10-inch pan, bake the cake for 35 minutes; a 9-inch pan takes 40 minutes. The cake will be soft when it comes out of the oven; it firms up as it cools.

A spring form pan is recommended because it has detachable sides so the torte can be removed without flipping it. You could also use a regular pan or a Pyrex baking dish and not remove the torte. (Serve pieces straight from the pan.)

Yield: Twelve servings

Deli Cheesecake

This is a rich, delicious cheesecake, New York deli style. It makes a good alternative to the standard layer cake for birthdays.

1¼ cup graham cracker crumbs (16 crackers — or a ready-made graham cracker crust.)	1 cup sugar
	2 teaspoons grated lemon peel
2 tablespoons sugar	3 eggs
3 tablespoons butter, melted	¼ teaspoon vanilla
2 8-ounce packages plus 1 3-ounce package cream cheese, softened	1 can cherry or blueberry pie filling or 1 cup dairy sour cream, for topping

1. Preheat the oven to 350 degrees. Stir together the graham crackers, 2 tablespoons of sugar and melted butter.

2. Press the crumbs into a 9-inch pan. Bake this crust 10 minutes, then cool.

3. Reduce the heat to 300 degrees. Beat the cream cheese; when it is whipped, add 1 cup of sugar and beat the mixture until it is fluffy.

4. Add the lemon peel and vanilla.

5. Beat in one egg at a time.

6. Pour this mixture into the cooled crumb crust; bake the cake one hour, until the center is firm.

7. Cool the cake to room temperature.

Yield: Twelve servings

OTHER GOODIES

These recipes don't fall into the baked goods categories, but they're too good to omit. Here you'll find a quick-and-easy recipe for an unusual jelly, and two dynamite punches.

Myra's Jalapeño Jelly

Myra Griffin serves this spicy jelly at her restaurant; it was so popular she began selling jars of it for people to take home. I'd been buying Myra's jelly for years when I finally got up the nerve to make it myself. I found it's incredibly easy and quick to make, and the bright green jars make great Christmas presents (see page 83). You can also substitute all red peppers and make a beautiful red jelly—and you won't need food coloring. (Myra buys lots of peppers in the summer and freezes some of them to make jelly in later months.) Serve pepper jelly with cream cheese on a mild cracker.

3 to 5 fresh jalapeño peppers (depending on how hot you want the jelly)	3 to 4 green bell peppers
	1 package powdered Sure-Jell
1 to 2 banana peppers	4 cups sugar
2 cayenne peppers	green food coloring
1 birdseed pepper	6 pint canning jars with self-sealing lids
½ cup cider vinegar	

1. Submerge jars in water in a large enamel pot; bring the water to a full boil. Allow it to boil for 10 minutes. Boil more water in a teapot and pour it over the lids. (Do not boil the lids.)

2. Cut the stems off the jalapeño, banana, cayenne and birdseed peppers, but leave the seeds in. Chop the peppers coarsely.

3. Put the peppers in the blender with the cider vinegar; grind them until they are fine.

4. Seed and chop the bell peppers; add enough peppers to make 4 cups of pepper mash. Blend.

5. Transfer the pepper mash to a large saucepan; add Sure-Jell while the peppers are still cool.

Herbal vinegars and jellies are surprisingly easy to make, and
they keep on giving over time. Pictured left to right: rosemary
and tarragon vinegars and peach, jalapeño and cherry jellies.

6. Heat the mixture on high, stirring constantly, until the mixture reaches a full boil. Add sugar and a few drops of green food coloring.

7. Boil the jelly for 2 minutes, stirring constantly, then pour it into the sterilized jars. (Tongs are helpful for removing jars and lids from scalding water.) Wipe the jar rims to remove any stray jelly; seal the jars and add homemade labels.

Myra's combination of peppers is designed to create a first, middle, and late "hot." If other peppers are unavailable, you can use jalapeños only, but never more than five unless you're a fire-eater. Increase the number of green peppers to make 4 cups of pepper mash.

Yield: Six (pint) jars of jelly

Cranberry Punch

This makes a great holiday punch as is, or mixed with rum. (The recipe is for a concentrate: you add hot water to serve.)

1 pound cranberries	2 6-ounce cans orange
4 cups water	juice concentrate
2 sticks cinnamon	1 cup sugar
6 whole cloves	1 bottle viejo rum
2 6-ounce cans lemonade	(optional)
concentrate	

1. Combine the cranberries, water, cinnamon and cloves in a saucepan.
2. Bring this mixture to a boil; boil for 20 minutes.
3. Run the mixture through a cheesecloth or sieve.
4. Add the sugar and the lemonade and orange juice concentrates; mix these ingredients well. Also add the rum, if you're using it.
5. This is your concentrate. To make punch, add 3 cups of hot water to 1 cup of concentrate.

Hot, Mulled Cider

Give guests a wonderfully warm welcome in the fall and winter months by serving them this spicy cider.

½ gallon cider	5 cloves
1 cinnamon stick	juice of one lemon
1 teaspoon whole allspice	

1. Place allspice and cloves in a tea ball; combine all the ingredients in a large pot.
2. Simmer for at least 15 minutes.

MEALS

As I said earlier in this chapter, giving a dinner party for a group of close friends isn't usually thought of as a gift, but it may be the best thing you can give — especially if you're chronically short on time to spend with others. Accordingly, I've included some of my favorite menus for entertaining: an Italian dinner, a Southern barbeque and a Mexican buffet.

To make entertaining more fun and less nerve-wracking, do as much preparation as possible the day — or days — before. (Make the dessert, bread and sauces, clean the house, set the table, etc.) Also, when cooking several things at once, try making a master list that organizes all tasks or operations on a timeline. That way, you'll know exactly when to do what, and will have more time to spend with your guests.

ITALIAN DINNER

This makes an elegant sit-down dinner. Serve with red wine.

- Stuffed Shells
- Zucchini Sauted in Wine
- Herbed Tomatoes
- Garlic Bread
- Tossed Salad with Vinagrette
- Spumoni or Sherbet

Stuffed Shells

This dramatic dish is always a crowd pleaser. Ideally, you'll prepare the spaghetti sauce the day before; you can also substitute a ready-made sauce, if time is limited. But no matter what sauce you use, try adding a cup of orange juice and a teaspoon of fennel or anise to get the tangy taste of this one!

2 10-ounce packages	shell macaroni
frozen chopped spinach	pinch of basil
½ pound sweet Italian	2 eggs
sausage	2 cups grated mozzerella
1 quart spaghetti sauce	cheese
(see recipe below or use	½ cup shredded
commercial sauce)	provolone cheese
12 ounce package jumbo	(optional)

15 ounces part skim ricotta	3 cloves garlic, crushed
3 tablespoons chopped onion	¼ teaspoon allspice
	½ cup Parmesan cheese

1. Thaw the packages of frozen spinach in a sink full of hot water.
2. Put 5 to 6 quarts of water in a pot on the stove to boil, adding a pinch of dried basil.
3. Crumble up the Italian sausage in a skillet and cook it on medium heat. Once the sausage is brown, drain off the fat and place the sausage on paper towels.
4. In a saucepan, heat the spaghetti sauce (see recipe below) and the sausage. Cover this mixture and reduce the heat. Allow it to simmer for 15 minutes to a half hour.
5. Meanwhile, place the thawed spinach in a strainer and press out the excess moisture by hand. Let it continue to drain until you're ready to mix up the filling.
6. When the pot of water reaches a rapid boil, add the shells a few at a time, so the water continues to bubble. Boil the shells, uncovered, for about 10 minutes, stirring occasionally. *Do not overcook the shells.* These shells should be al dente. Drain them immediately and set the colander aside.
7. In a large bowl, beat the eggs slightly. Add the mozzerella, provolone and ricotta cheeses, chopped onion, garlic and allspice, then the spinach, stirring until the ingredients are well mixed.
8. Preheat the oven to 350 degrees. Pour half the sauce in the bottom of a 3-quart casserole.
9. Stuff each shell with 2 spoonfuls of spinach and cheese filling. Arrange the shells in a single layer in the casserole dish. Tuck in the remaining shells.
10. Pour the remaining sauce on top of the shells; sprinkle with parmesan. Bake at 350 degrees for 30 minutes.

Yield: Six servings

With a hot glue gun, rocks and magnets, make gifts to hold up notes on the refrigerator.

Spaghetti Sauce

1 15-ounce can tomato sauce	4 cloves garlic, finely sliced or crushed
1 6-ounce can tomato paste	1 tablespoon basil
1 cup orange juice	2 teaspoons oregano
1 onion, diced	1 teaspoon salt
	1 teaspoon fennel or anise seed

Combine all the ingredients in a saucepan. Bring the mixture to a boil, then reduce the heat to low and simmer for at least ½ hour.

Zucchini Sauted in Wine

This is a tangy side dish that complements any meal, whether you're entertaining or not. And this is a tasty way to use up excess zucchini in the summertime, too.

4 cups zucchini, sliced	2 cloves garlic
3 tablespoons olive oil	3 tablespoons white wine
1 cup onion, chopped	

1. Heat the olive oil in a heavy skillet; saute the onion and garlic until they are golden.
2. Add sliced zucchini and cover the pan; cook for about 6 minutes, shaking the pan regularly to pre-

vent sticking.

3. Cook the zucchini until it is tender, then remove the lid and add the wine; cook for 2 more minutes.

Yield: Six servings

Herbed Tomatoes

This is an easy, delicious way to serve tomatoes. If you can get fresh herbs, so much the better.

6 Italian plum tomatoes (or 3 regular)	¼ teaspoon oregano
1 teaspoon dried thyme	freshly ground pepper
½ teaspoon basil	salt

1. Wash the tomatoes and slice them thinly. Arrange them on a plate.
2. Crush the herbs between your fingers as you sprinkle them over the tomato slices.
3. Grind pepper over the tomatoes, and add salt to taste.

Yield: Six servings

SOUTHERN STYLE BARBEQUE

This is a fun summer alternative to the usual steaks or burgers. For this meal, in addition to the recipes that follow, try the corn bread recipe on the back of the Quaker Corn Meal box, and the pecan pie recipe on the bottle of Karo corn syrup. The pie is incredibly easy and good!

- •Barbequed Ribs
- •Red Beans and Rice
- •Cole Slaw
- •Corn Bread
- •Pecan Pie with vanilla ice cream

Barbequed Ribs

This sauce is spicy and not too hot—serve with Tobasco for people who like to "burn." Save unused sauce in the refrigerator; it's also good for barbequing chicken. The secret of this recipe is boiling the ribs in beer!

2 slabs of ribs, country style cut	1 cup brown sugar
6 pack of beer	½ cup lemon juice
1 cup honey	1 cup Worcestershire sauce
½ cup prepared mustard	2 cups catsup

3 cloves garlic, crushed	1 teaspoon cumin
1 tablespoon dried onion flakes	1 teaspoon Tobasco sauce
1 teaspoon black pepper	½ teaspoon cayenne

1. Mix the honey and mustard until smooth; add the brown sugar, lemon juice, catsup and Worcestershire sauce. Add the spices and blend well. (If possible, mix up this sauce the night before, so the flavors can mingle.)
2. Cut the ribs apart so they'll sit in a large kettle; cover with the beer.
3. Bring the ribs and beer to a boil; reduce the heat and simmer, covered, for 35 minutes.
4. Start some coals in an outdoor grill.
5. When the ribs are light brown, remove them from the beer and smother them with barbeque sauce.
6. Grill the ribs quickly over hot coals.

Some folks would see only two slabs of ribs as slim pickin's for six people, but served with beans and rice, it's just fine, and helps keep the cost down. However, there is enough sauce to cover several more slabs of ribs, should you care to make them.

Yield: Six servings

Red Beans and Rice

In the South, people make a whole meal out of this dish. It's delicious and nutritious. In this menu, beans and rice help stretch the ribs.

2½ cups kidney beans, soaked overnight or quick soaked	3 bay leaves
	1 teaspoon Tobasco sauce
2 ham hocks	1 teaspoon thyme
2 cups sliced smoked sausage (precooked)	1 teaspoon sugar
	1 teaspoon cumin
1 cup chopped celery, tops and all	½ teaspoon oregano
	½ teaspoon cayenne
1 bell pepper, chopped	½ teaspoon black pepper
1 large onion, chopped	¼ teaspoon red pepper
5 cloves garlic, diced or pressed	flakes ("birdseed" peppers)
	2 cups rice

1. Place presoaked beans in a large kettle; cover them with water.
2. Add all the remaining ingredients *except* the rice and allow them to simmer for several hours, stirring

For soft, mottled images like the ones on this popcorn tin,
dip a natural sea sponge in acrylic paint and dab it onto a base-
coated surface. Sponge on several different colors to create
deep, rich shades.

them occasionally. Add more water as it becomes necessary.

3. When the beans are soft, prepare the rice according to the directions on the package.

To quick soak beans, place them in a large pot. Pour in enough water to cover the beans by 2 inches. Bring the beans to a boil; allow them to boil for 2 minutes. Remove the beans from the heat; cover them and allow them to soak for 1 hour.

Yield: Ten servings

MEXICAN BUFFET

Many people love Mexican food, or spicy food in general—you've probably guessed that I fall into that category! Although only the salsa and the cookies are authentically Mexican, this meal has a south of the border appeal that makes it a real fiesta.

- •Salsa and Chips
- •Hot Stuff Calzone
- •Red Cabbage Salad
- •Mexican Wedding Cookies (see page 77) and Frozen Yogurt

Salsa

This is a medium range salsa with lots of flavor.

6 plum tomatoes (or 3 regular sized), diced	1 can green chilis, minced
5 cloves garlic, minced	juice of one lime
3 green onions, sliced	1 tablespoon fresh cilantro
1 jalapeño pepper, seeded	1 teaspoon salt

1. Combine all the ingredients—including any juice from the tomatoes—in a bowl. Stir lightly.
2. Refrigerate the salsa until ready to serve.

Hot Stuff Calzone

Be forewarned: This recipe is hot! But because any combination of peppers can be used, it's easy to tone it down. For instance, substitute pepperoncinis for the tiny hots to experience a dramatically milder dish. However, I've found that even people who don't like hot food find this dish irresistible. Maybe it's the jelly roll shape, and the kaleidoscope of colors—whatever, this is my most asked for recipe of all time.

Also, please note that this is the "ultimate" recipe you have in your hands. Ideally all these ingredients are included, but in reality they seldom are. To simplify the recipe, just make sure there are about ⅔ cup hot pickled peppers, ¾ cup sweet peppers, and 2 cups cheese. (I often use just mozzerella and parmesan.) The olives, however, are indispensable.

½ cup hot pepper rings	½ cup parmesan, grated
5 tiny hots, sliced or 6 jalapeños, sliced	¼ cup aged provolone (or smoked mozzerella)
⅓ cup green olives, sliced	1 teaspoon crushed red pepper flakes
⅓ cup black olives, sliced	
¼ cup green pepper, chopped	1 teaspoon ground black pepper
¼ cup sweet red pepper, chopped	1 teaspoon basil
	1 teaspoon oregano
¼ cup sweet yellow pepper, chopped	2 tablespoons dried onion flakes
2 tablespoons olive oil	dough for 1 pizza crust (See recipe below or use commercial dough, sold in the dairy case at supermarkets.)
6 cloves garlic, sliced fine	
6 dried tomatoes, slivered (optional)	
¾ cup mozzerella, keeping some bigger slices intact	

1. Preheat the oven to 350 degrees. Put the hot peppers and olives in a strainer; squeeze them to remove any excess liquid. Allow them to drain while you prepare the other ingredients.
2. Saute the sweet peppers in olive oil until they are translucent. Drain them on paper towels.
3. Combine the cheeses in a large bowl. Stir in the red pepper flakes, black pepper, basil, oregano and dried onion flakes. Set this mixture aside.
4. Roll out the pizza dough to form a large rectangle, approximately 18 × 12 inches.
5. Give the hot peppers a final squeeze to eliminate any moisture, then stir them into the bowl of cheeses. Add the sweet peppers and mix well. This is your filling.
6. Spread the filling evenly across the dough, leaving a little space around all the edges. Fold over the ends of the dough, then roll it up like a jelly roll, pinching the ends as you go. (See illustration on page 89.) If the dough should break open as you're

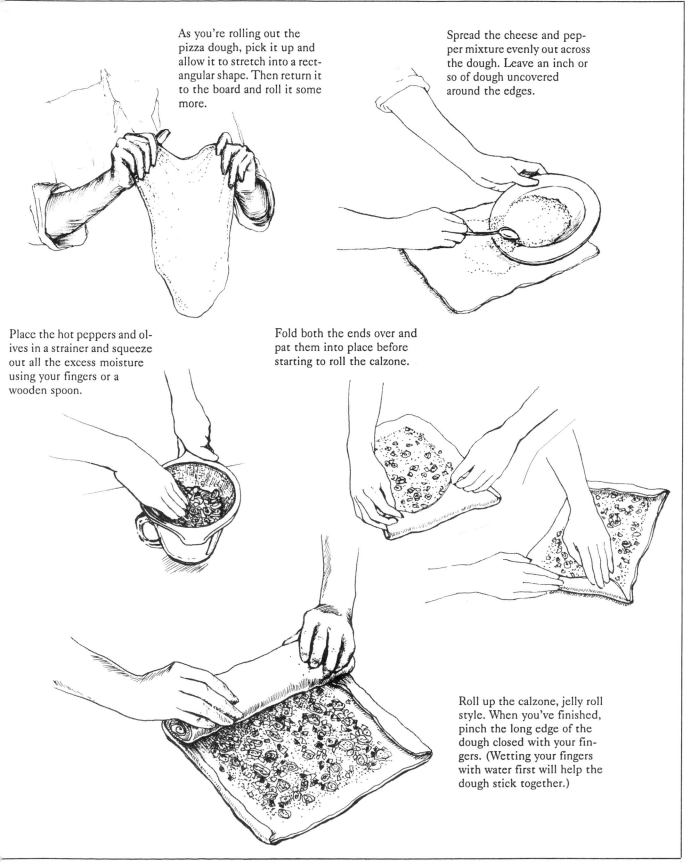

As you're rolling out the pizza dough, pick it up and allow it to stretch into a rectangular shape. Then return it to the board and roll it some more.

Spread the cheese and pepper mixture evenly out across the dough. Leave an inch or so of dough uncovered around the edges.

Place the hot peppers and olives in a strainer and squeeze out all the excess moisture using your fingers or a wooden spoon.

Fold both the ends over and pat them into place before starting to roll the calzone.

Roll up the calzone, jelly roll style. When you've finished, pinch the long edge of the dough closed with your fingers. (Wetting your fingers with water first will help the dough stick together.)

rolling, simply pull it together with your fingers.

7. Brush drops of water along the long side of the roll to help the dough bond. Seal it by pinching, like you'd crimp a pie crust.

8. Place the seam side of the roll down on a greased baking sheet and poke holes in the dough with a fork.

9. Bake the roll at 350 degrees for 25 to 30 minutes, until the crust is golden brown.

Yield: Six servings

Pizza Dough for Hot Stuff Calzone

1 envelope active dry yeast	2 tablespoons olive oil
1 warm beer	3¼ to 4 cups flour
1 teaspoon salt	

Dissolve the yeast in the beer. Stir in the salt and olive oil. Gradually add the flour to this mixture. Beat until the dough is smooth, adding more flour as necessary to manage the dough. Knead the dough on a lightly floured board until it is smooth and elastic. Brush the top of the dough with olive oil, cover it lightly, and let it rise in a warm place until it is doubled in bulk. After the dough rises, divide it in half, then roll each half into a ball. Roll the dough out as described above. (Freeze the other half, unless you are making two calzones.)

Yield: Two crusts

Red Cabbage Salad

This marinated salad adds color and crunch to any meal, and makes an exotic substitute for cole slaw. The sesame oil gives it a nutty taste, and the mustard gives it tang.

1 head red cabbage, chopped	1 clove garlic, crushed
2 carrots, coarsely grated	1 tablespoon Dijon mustard
½ red onion, sliced into thin crescents	1 teaspoon Oriental sesame oil
½ cup olive oil	salt
½ cup red wine vinegar	pepper

1. Combine cabbage, carrots and onion in a bowl.

2. In a separate container, combine the remaining ingredients and stir them well to mix. (I use the blender.)

3. Pour the marinade over the cabbage mixture, stirring well. Cover and refrigerate for at least an hour before serving.

Yield: Eight servings

Topiary trees can be made in all sizes and with materials to
reflect any season and complement any decor. Simply hot glue
dried flowers to a Styrofoam ball. Add a stick and a flowerpot
for a unique floral creation. (See page 37 for instructions.)

LITTLE GIFTS
THAT MEAN A LOT

*S*ome people are exasperatingly tough to figure out when it comes to what they like. For these folks, I sometimes like to cover my bets by giving them several small gifts, each individually wrapped, in one large gift box or basket.

This chapter covers a lot of smaller possibilities that may work for those hard to please people on your list. Most of these gifts are exceptionally easy to make, since they're assembled from materials you already have on hand. Armed with a glue gun and a few simple craft techniques such as decoupage and paint manipulations (ragging, striating, etc.), explained in the How-To section, you can make a wealth of gifts.

Little gift ideas range from photo albums to flowerpots, from desk accessories and hand-printed stationery to jewelry — and jewelry runs the gamut from button pins to feather earrings, from safety pin bracelets to corn necklaces. You're sure to find projects suitable for many different people in this chapter.

IDEAS

This section is a potpourri of gift ideas that can be adapted in a variety of ways for totally different looks. Many of these ideas can be put together in just a few minutes, provided you have the materials on hand.

Refrigerator Magnets: With small magnets and a glue gun, you can make these downhome accessories out of just about anything: shells, rocks, buttons, fossils, novelties, old jewelry — you name it! Simply glue the magnet onto the back of the object and you have an instant gift.

Coordinated Desk Accessories: People who work at home appreciate colorful gifts for their offices. Try decorating a blotter, pencil holder, wastebasket, noteboard and letter holder with fabric, old maps, collage, yarn or paint. Use a glue-on, decoupage-like technique (described below for maps) to attach fabric and paper; don't forget marbleized paper and wrapping paper as possible materials. Or apply paint in different ways for a multitude of special effects. (See the Special Finishes entry in the How-To section.)

Maps are a traditionally masculine treatment for desk accessories. Gather old road maps or maps like those provided each month in *National Geographic*. Measure your wastebasket, pencil holder and blotter holder, then cut the maps to size. In a dishpan, mix white glue with a small amount of water — ½ inch to 1 inch in depth. Dip a map in quickly, then apply it to the surface, smoothing out wrinkles and air bubbles with your fingers. Allow your surface to dry on waxed paper or a sheet of plastic wrapped cardboard; then shellac it with water-based varnish.

Yet another idea is to decorate desk accessories by spray painting around objects such as leaves or doilies — see the How-To section of Chapter Seven for instructions.

Custom-printed Stationery: Print stationery and envelopes using shapes cut out of sponge, or direct impressions of leaves, flowers, vegetables, whatever. (See the How-To section in Chapter Four for printing advice.) For example, I've made stationery using an old wooden printing block I purchased at an antique store. Purchase a box of stationery to decorate, or put together your own sets of envelopes and paper after purchasing them separately, in bulk, from an office supply store. Then use printer's inks or acrylic paints to print the paper.

Handmade Paper: For friends who love to write, try making sheets of paper. Handmade paper has a tactile and visual appeal that makes commercially manufactured paper pale by comparison. You can add dried flower petals, herbs and spices, coffee grounds, glitter or small bits of cloth into the pulp mix for extra special papers. (See page 106 for instructions.)

Decorated Notepads and Blank Books: A writer friend of mine is a great fan of collage, so I made her a personalized notebook decorated with pictures cut from old magazines, then shellacked. The key to effective collage is to make sure the pictures interrelate, which can be accomplished by coordinating the colors, overlapping some of the pictures, and cutting out shapes so that some of the background picture shows through.

Decorated Planters: Potted plants are gifts that keep on giving throughout the year, and they're that much more special when you give them in a hand-decorated pot. Plain ceramic flowerpots can be transformed with paint into one-of-a-kind decorating accents. You can embellish planters in a variety of ways — with spray on webbing, stencils, sponge painting and more. See the Special Finishes entry on pages 103-105 for details. In addition, you'll find several rustic twig planter ideas in Chapter Three.

You can make one-of-a-kind accessories in minutes using old buttons. All you have to do is arrange several buttons in a grouping, glue them together, and add jewelry findings.

Tari Sasser Jacober made this unique jewelry set out of Fimo modeling compound, which doesn't require firing. Once the design is formed, you just pop the jewelry in the oven for fifteen minutes.

I used fabric markers to decorate these tennis shoes for a friend. With bright colors and your own design, you can create snazzy shoes in minutes.

Picture Frames and Mirrors: Frames can be finished with just about anything—pinecones, shells, pebbles, memorabilia (see my frame on page 97), buttons, beads, pasta, ribbons, marbleized or cut paper, fabric, glitter, confetti or special paint finishes. (See the How-To section for a variety of attractive finishes.) Decoupage old picture frames with paper

you've marbleized yourself, or buy a book of ready to use marbleized papers. (Dover Books publishes one that consists of twelve full-color 11½ × 18-inch sheets, by Judith B. Saurman and Judith A. Pierce, available for about four dollars.) You can also use unusual wrapping paper to cover a frame, or even handmade paper (see the How-To section for details).

Pinecone frames are great for housing watercolors or line drawings. Simply use hot glue to attach small pinecones onto an old frame. And memorabilia frames look good with heirloom photos or family portraits. Gather small mementos—earrings, buttons, shells, rocks, gumball treasures, old diaper pins—and glue them onto an old frame. If you're loath to part with your own memorabilia, look for whimsical trinkets at garage sales and second-hand stores.

Painted Tile Trivets: Hand-painted tiles make great hostess or housewarming gifts. Individual tiles are available at craft stores or tile suppliers—sometimes tile stores will even give you a few samples for free (check your Yellow Pages under Tile—Ceramic for dealers). Draw your design with a chinagraph pencil, then color it in using model paints or enamels. Once the paint is dry, protect your design with a coat of ceramic varnish.

Shell Cocktail Toothpicks: Here's another great hostess gift idea. Collect small shells, or buy them at a craft or hobby store, then use hot glue to attach them to the ends of toothpicks for unique cocktail servers. (If you gather your own shells, place them in boiling water for 15 minutes to sterilize them.) You may want to shellac shells for extra shine. Place in a small, decorated box for giving.

Decorated Boxes: These are great gifts for hard to please people, because who ever has enough storage? Boxes can be used to hold jewelry, pocket change and keys, recipes, tissues, paper clips, pencils, art supplies, hats, scarves, gloves—you could even decorate a lunch box. Consider using decoupage, autumn leaves (see the How-To section in Chapter Three), shells, rocks, junk jewelry, maps (see the Desk Accessories entry earlier in this section) or just paint on your box (see the Special Finishes in the How-To section for details).

Papier-Mâché Napkin Rings, Bowls or Trays: If you remember papier-mâché from elementary school, you may be surprised by its range of possibilities. Start with cardboard forms, hot glued together (for instance, a strip of cardboard hot glued into a circle for a napkin ring or bracelet, a piece of plywood with a cardboard rim hot glued around the edges for a tray) then cover the forms with strips of newspaper that have been dipped in a flour and water paste. Apply several layers of the newspaper, then allow the object to dry. Coat with gesso and paint with colorful acrylics in fun designs to finish.

Painted Jars: To personalize small gifts, try painting jars to match. Hand-painted jars are great for presenting friends with dried herbs from your garden, homemade jams, candies, nuts, seeds, herbal vinegars, potpourri, even seashells — virtually any gift item that can be contained in a jar or bottle. Jar decorations can be simple or elaborate, graphic or floral, monochromatic or multicolored. Sometimes the shape of the bottle will give you an idea for a design; other times the gift will suggest a pattern. Of course you'll consider the recipient's taste and favorite colors, but don't overlook the color of the gift itself. Work with colors that contrast with the contents of the jar if you want your decorative painting to be visible. (See the How-To section for more specific instructions.)

Punched Tin Candle Holders and Jar Lids: Paint old tin cans then punch them with holes for rustic candle holders that give off points of light; or punch holes in jar lids to create decorative tops for gifts of candy or potpourri. You could punch designs like swirls or stars, or actual pictures such as teddy bears, hearts or Santas. Simply draw a pattern onto tracing or typing paper, then use masking tape to hold it onto the lid or side of the can. Place the lid on a piece of wood and use a nail to pound holes, following your design; change the nail if the point becomes dull. Repunch holes if they seem indistinct. Remove your pattern and tape. If you want, you can paint the area inside the punches to further distinguish your design.

Mobiles and Wind Chimes: You can make beautiful mobiles and eloquent wind chimes out of found materials for mere pennies. Simply drill holes in the objects, thread them on fishing line or copper wire, and suspend them from your base. For instance, hang shells from a piece of driftwood so that they knock together in the breeze, or flatten old silverware with a hammer and hang it from an old metal colander.

You can make a fun frame out of anything that can be glued down. This frame was decorated with small mementos, including earrings, buttons, shells, rocks and gumball treasures.

Spray paint over doilies to create unique wrapping papers (see page 113), then top packages with small bouquets called tussie mussies (see page 37) to add style to your gift-giving.

Glue on confetti or potpourri. Print with a sponge, celery or rubber stamps. Make a collage box. Use your imagination to come up with unusual gift wrap ideas such as these. (All the techniques are described in Chapter Seven, Finishing Touches.)

One of my favorites is a bunch of rusty metal stuff hung from an old gas stove burner that I gave to my father to hang in his garden. (See the photo on page 92 for a variation of the rusty stuff mobile theme.)

Personalized Photo Album: If you're a shutter-bug, this makes a great gift for family members and close friends. Simply go through all your old snapshots and choose pictures around a theme (i.e., "history of our family," or "a variety of vacations," "holidays through the years," or "funny faces we have made"). Arrange them in an interesting sequence in a store-bought album or put together one on your own using a loose-leaf notebook, construction paper, and those little corner holders for holding photos in place. An alternate idea is to photocopy some choice pictures then use a photo transfer medium to print them on T-shirts. (See the How-To section in Chapter Four for instructions.)

Play Dough: A great gift for small children, especially festive when presented in gaily decorated containers (save old cottage cheese or other airtight containers, then paint them with colorful designs). This recipe comes from Jill Dunford's book, *Teach Me Mommy*, a preschool learning guide. To make play dough, mix 1 cup flour, ½ cup salt, 1 tablespoon alum, 1 cup water, 1 tablespoon oil, and a few drops of food coloring in a saucepan. Cook over medium heat, stirring constantly, until the mixture reaches the consistency of mashed potatoes. Remove from heat and add 2 tablespoons vanilla. Stored in an airtight container, play dough will keep for about a month.

Painted Tennis Shoes: A fun gift for kids and playful adults, tennis shoes can be painted with wild abstract designs or with animal faces. Start with canvas tennis shoes; wash and dry them to remove sizing. Lightly sketch out your design with a pencil, then color it in with permanent markers or fabric paints (see the photo on page 96).

Jewelry Ideas

Button Jewelry: There's something intriguing about buttons. Before 1925, when the zipper was invented, buttons were universal. Maybe that's why there are so many old buttons still around. Making button jewelry is a nifty way to use those beautiful antique buttons you inherited from your grand-mother. Even if you don't have a button collection, you can check second-hand and discount stores for unusual buttons. And don't forget your own sewing box. You'll be amazed at how quickly you can put together attractive coordinated jewelry—for practically pennies! See the How-To Section for specifics.

Corn Necklace: These Southwestern necklaces can be dyed a rainbow of hues. Just buy large-kernel corn at a feed store, then dye it in an old coffee can using concentrated liquid dye. Add just enough water to cover the corn. Let it sit for about twenty-four hours, or until color is slightly darker than desired, stirring occasionally. To speed up the process, heat the can of dye and corn in a larger pan of boiling water on the stove, double-boiler style.

Drain off the dye and rinse the corn thoroughly in hot water, until the water runs clear. Spread kernels out on paper towels to dry, then use a Yankee hand drill, a small nail, or a darning needle to poke holes in the ends. Thread a leather strip or length of elastic through the holes; knot the ends to secure. (You can dye the leather strip the same color as the corn, but only dip it briefly or the leather will disintegrate.)

Even if you don't dye the corn, it must be soaked or heated to be soft enough to pierce. To attach chili peppers, poke holes and thread them as you did the corn. Then use craft cement to secure them to neighboring kernels, as well as to repair rips in the chilis themselves, which are brittle. To finish, coat the peppers with a water-based varnish.

Wrapped Bracelets: Anything "twistable" should be considered for bracelet possibilities. This includes embroidery floss, wire, ribbon, and raffia (a durable dried grasslike material available at hobby stores). Make patterns using different colors of the same material—copper and gold wire, or red, white and blue embroidery floss, for instance. Or be innovative and experiment with different combinations of materials. Secure the ends by knotting or gluing.

Safety Pin Bracelet: Who'd have thought you could turn safety pins into stunning jewelry—in less than an hour! I've seen these bracelets sold for as much as thirty dollars in gift shops, but they can be made for less than five dollars, if you use the inexpensive beads sold by the bag in craft stores. Designer glass beads, on the other hand, can cost as much as fifty cents a piece, increasing the cost of the bracelet dramatically—but it's still much cheaper to assemble one yourself than to buy an equivalent bracelet. See the How-To section for specifics.

Decoupage Bangle Bracelets: Either classic decoupage, with clearly defined pictures set against a stained wood background, or a more papier-maché-like collage treatment can be used to create an attractive gift, tailor-made for the recipient.

Purchase wooden or plastic bangle bracelets at a craft, discount or thrift store. (For classic decoupage, use a wooden bracelet base. Apply a wood stain and allow it to dry thoroughly before proceeding.) For the papier-maché method, you can use plastic bracelets, available for as little as twenty-five cents each at thrift stores. See the How-To section for decoupage instructions.

Folded Paper Jewelry: Use watercolor paper or the paper ribbon sold in craft stores to make elegant jewelry in a jiffy. The paper can be cut, folded or gathered accordian-style into fans; it can be painted, collaged or embellished with glitter and "jewels," then shellacked, to create fantastic accessories. See the How-To section for instructions.

Feather Earrings: Feathers have a sensual appeal that has endured since time immemorial; feather earrings make great gifts for women with a taste for the unusual. Probably one of the first "accessories" to be worn by humans, feathers are festive and are frequently used on costumes for Carnival, Mardi Gras and all sorts of parades. An incredible array of colors and shapes of feathers are sold in sporting goods stores to be used in tying flies for fishing. All you need to do is add a few beads and jewelry findings to create unique, exotic accessories. See the How-To section for information on working with feathers.

Beaded Jewelry: Like feathers, beads are an ancient form of adornment. They come in virtually all sizes, shapes and styles, and are made of everything from shell and bone to plastic and metal. Beautiful necklaces and bracelets can be made from strands of beads—easily, quickly, and usually quite inexpensively. (Except when you fall in love with beads that cost twenty-five cents a piece. To help cut costs, always be on the lookout for old jewelry that can be taken apart and recycled.)

To string beads, all you need is a beading needle, a length of nylon, beading wire, waxed thread or elastic, a selection of beads, and perhaps a barrel clasp or some other fastener. Create a pattern of three different colored beads, or use various sizes and shapes of beads on the same piece. For a more elegant look, include several strands on the same necklace, joined gracefully by a clasp.

Fish Lure Jewelry: It's worth a trip to the sporting goods store just to see the fishing lures. They range from wacky and wild to relatively conservative, and most can be made into earrings. Many lures come equipped with beads and "spinners"—little metal ovals that twirl around in a way that fish find irresistable. (As an earring, the spinner will jingle softly with movement.)

To make earrings, just buy two lures of the same type, snip off the hooks with side cutting pliers, and attach pierced earring wires. (See the illustration on page 103.) If you know a woman who likes to fish— or if the man in her life does—try this alluring gift idea.

Shell Earrings: Like feathers and beads, shells are another ancient ornament. You can use shells collected during vacations at the beach or buy them at a craft or nature store. (This second option offers the

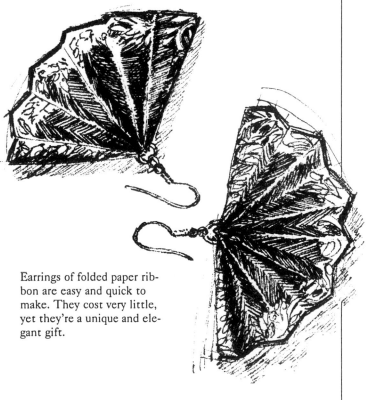

Earrings of folded paper ribbon are easy and quick to make. They cost very little, yet they're a unique and elegant gift.

advantage of uniformity—shells have already been presorted and grouped.)

Some shells are thin enough to be pierced with a darning needle, but most require a drill. Use the finest drill bit you have, and be aware that shells sometimes crack just as you finish drilling. Attach findings directly if possible; otherwise, twist wire into a loop and attach earring wire to that.

Modeling Compound Jewelry: Making jewelry out of colored modeling compound is as easy and fun as playing with clay! It's available in a variety of hues, and the colors can be mixed to create your own special blends. Because this medium is so flexible, you can experiment with several different ideas before committing yourself to one. Nothing is final until you decide it is. Your finished designs are made permanent by baking for 15 minutes in the oven. See the How-To section for more specific instructions.

Christmas Package Pin and Earrings: Festive jewelry makes a great Christmas gift. Ready-made miniature packages are made by Westrim; you simply glaze the packages with varnish, and attach pin backs and earring findings. Or you can construct a small package by folding watercolor paper into a rectangle,

wrapping it with festive paper, and tying on a tiny satin ribbon. Glaze with a water-based varnish such as Ceramcoat or Envirotex; then glue on findings.

Roses and Lace Barrette: Romantic accessories combine ribbons, lace and roses to make an ultrafeminine statement. Arrange the lace or crochet trim in an attractive shape so that it covers the barrette: fan shapes, bow ties and rectangles are a few possibilities. Tie a multilooped bow out of ⅛-inch satin ribbon (use about 2 yards). Glue this in the center of the lace. After you've arranged the bow and lace satisfactorily, apply a fabric stiffener such as Stiffy to them and allow it to dry. Then glue a 1-inch rose made of satin, porcelain or silk in the center of the bow, and hot glue a barrette to the back.

Found Object Jewelry: So far we've made jewelry out of paper, feathers, buttons, beads, safety pins, shells—even fish lures. Just about anything that has a hole in it or can be glued onto a backing has the potential to be made into jewelry. That includes, but isn't limited to, children's party favors, accessories for miniatures collections, coins, rocks and fossils. Use your imagination to come up with ideas tailored specifically to the recipient's taste.

It's worth a trip to the sporting goods store just to see the fishing lures. Many of them come equipped with beads and "spinners" that make them perfect for funky jewelry. Simply snip off the hooks with a pair of side cutting pliers and add earring wires. For larger lures, add a jump ring and cord to make a fun necklace.

HOW-TO'S

The crafts described in this section run the gamut from paper folding and papier-maché to special painted finishes and jewelry making. These basic techniques can be used on a wide variety of projects, so don't limit yourself to my suggestions.

Decoupage

This simple technique looks great on bracelets, boxes and even furniture.

Step 1: To begin, cut pictures or patterns out of magazines or decoupage source books. Also, don't forget marbleized paper and wrapping paper as possible materials for decoupage.

Step 2: Thin white glue with some water. Dip the paper into this mixture, and then pull it through your fingers to remove the excess glue.

Step 3: Apply the paper carefully to the object, either by wrapping (for a pattern), or by placing individual images. Use a paintbrush to smooth out the glue. When the decoupage dries, apply at least five thin coats of a clear varnish, allowing each coat to dry thoroughly before adding the next.

Special Finishes

A little paint can go a long way if you apply it in special ways. Special finishes look good on plant containers, boxes, trays, picture frames, wooden jewelry, even gift wrap, and can be executed in a wide range of colors.

Mottling Technique: By dabbing a crumpled piece of plastic wrap into wet paint, you can create a wonderfully textured look, as I did on the popcorn tin on page 87. Here's how to do it:

1. Cover your work surface with newspaper. If necessary, use masking tape to protect the areas you don't want paint on (for example, to maintain a nice clean line on the inside lip of a flowerpot). Base coat the piece with enamel paint; once this dries, apply a second coat.

2. In a well-ventilated area, use a foam applicator (sponge brush) to apply your thinned-down paint or glaze in a contrasting color. Brush it on vertically, then spread it out horizontally, and finish by brushing vertically again. Before the glaze dries, crumple up a piece of plastic wrap and press it repeatedly against the surface to mottle the glaze. Once the wrap is covered with paint, begin with a new piece. When you've

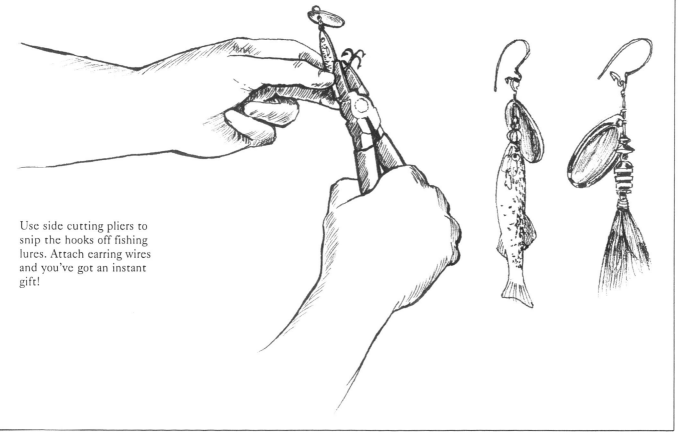

Use side cutting pliers to snip the hooks off fishing lures. Attach earring wires and you've got an instant gift!

Start collecting rusty nails and scraps of metal, and before long you'll be able to make a funky wind chime like this one. Or visit a scrap yard and stock up immediately! I used copper wire to connect the various pieces; the top was made from a steamer from an old cast iron pot.

covered the entire surface, set the object aside to dry.

3. Let the piece dry for 24 hours, then brush on several thin coats of varnish, allowing each to dry before applying the next.

Ragging: This soft, textural effect looks great on a variety of home accessories. Just apply a base coat to your surface, let it dry, then use a rag to apply a thin layer of glaze. Blot with a cotton rag. Even out any excess glaze with a stiff bristle brush. Or you can bunch up the rag and roll it through the glaze.

Combing: This technique looks good on band boxes and frames. Use a combing tool, or make your own by cutting "teeth" into a piece of cardboard. Apply a glaze of color over a contrasting base coat, and before the glaze dries, rake over it with the combing tool.

Sponging: Apply a base coat to your surface, then use a natural sea sponge and acrylic paint to dab on soft texture. Use three or four glaze colors for deeper, richer color. This finish looks great on planters, boxes, frames and lamp shades, as well as on the walls.

Striating: This subtle effect looks good on furniture and home accessories. First, apply a base coat to the object to be decorated. Once this dries, apply a glaze of color. Then drag steel wool through the glaze to create lots of little lines.

Pickling: This very easy and popular technique involves brushing thinned-down paint or a transparent pickling gel (Delta offers a variety of shades) onto raw wood, then rubbing most of the color off with a rag. The effect is subtle and elegant.

Webbing: Spray this finish on clothing or home accessories for a unique textural look. Manufactured by Carnival, webbing comes in a variety of colors, which can be used in combination or alone, over a base coat.

Checkerboard: Create a checkered finish on notebooks, planters, cannisters, tabletops and more. Simply cut strips of masking tape and place them vertically and horizontally on a base coated surface, leaving one inch spaces between the strips to form squares. Paint the squares a contrasting color to your base coat—black and white or black and red are classic combinations, but don't be afraid to play around with color. When the paint dries, remove the tape and touch up as needed.

Faux Granite: Using a product called Fleck Stone you can create faux granite surfaces on objects ranging from pencil boxes to vases, flowerpots, picture frames and more. Fleck Stone comes in fifteen shades, ranging from the sunbaked colors of the Southwest, to high-style metropolitan colors like Gotham Gray, and quarry colors, such as Ironstone. Fleck Stone is easy and fun to work with, and people love the way it looks.

You can also make your own granite-like finish using acrylic paints. Base coat your object in a warm neutral color. When this dries, make up a glaze by adding water to a mixture of burnt umber, raw umber, Payne's gray and titanium white. Apply this glaze with a bristle brush, then use a rag to absorb the excess water. With a damp natural sea sponge, dab more glaze onto the object; also dip the sponge in the individual colors. Use an old toothbrush to speckle the object with the individual colors by dipping the brush in thinned paint, then rub your thumb across the bristles to flick the paint lightly onto the object. Once the paint is dry, finish the object with several coats of varnish.

Painted Jars

Use old jars to give such gifts as food or potpourri a unique presentation—you create your own designs to suit the gift, the occasion and the recipient. You can use a paint brush to dab on small blobs of color; swirl on abstract designs; or create such seasonal motifs as hearts, flags or Santas. You could also try some of the special finishes just described. When giving gifts of dried herbs from my garden, I like to hand-paint small jars with a picture of the herb enclosed. Use oil-based markers, model paints or acrylics designed for use on glass. (Check the label and follow manufacturer's instructions.) Here are a few basic steps to follow:

Step 1: Collect empty glass jars of various shapes and sizes. Wash them thoroughly in hot water to remove the labels; then scrape off any residual glue with a knife. This glue is extremely gummy when fresh, but over time it becomes brittle and chips off easily. So, if possible, it's better to let your jars age for a few weeks.

Step 2: Some designs are basic enough to be painted freehand on the jar. You can just play around, have fun, and not worry too much about how it'll turn out. Others you'll want to plan a bit more. For these, first sketch your design on a piece of paper. If you find it isn't quite the right size for your jar, reduce or enlarge the pattern using a photocopy machine, or simply redraw it to scale. Then tape it, face out, to the inside of the jar to act as a guide while you paint. Carbon paper is also good for transferring intricate designs to jar lids.

Step 3: Now, using your pattern, paint your design. Various paints, both oil- and water-based, are suitable for use on glass. I've used both types of paints and been satisfied with the results. Oils tend to be more durable, but if you're working with children, water-based paints are preferable, since they're non-toxic and easy to clean up. Keep cotton swabs on hand for cleaning up any mistakes on the jar—you can dip the swabs in turpentine if working with oil paints, or water for acrylics.

Step 4: After 48 hours, heat harden the paint by placing the jar in a cold oven, then turning it on to 200 degrees. Turn the oven off after an hour, leaving the jar inside to cool. (Check manufacturer's instructions—many paints are not recommended for use on eating and drinking utensils, but as long as they're heat hardened, they're fine for decorative tableware. Most are washable in cool water and a gentle detergent, but not in the dishwasher.)

Step 5: Once the jars are dry, insert the gifts. Filling jars loosely often shows off the design better than stuffing them does. This is especially true with potpourri; if you pack the jar too full, the pattern won't show up as well. Lightly fluffing up the potpourri seems to work best.

Handmade Paper

Making paper is easy and fun to do. Handmade paper is popular with artsy types; its texture and subtle color appeal to sensual people. Homemade paper can be used to make unique gift tags, paper jewelry and stationery; unusual pieces can even be matted and framed as art. Recycle old envelopes, business cards, computer paper and stationery to make your pulp; add dried flowers, potpourri, coffee grounds, glitter and bits of cloth for special effects.

Step 1: Tear your paper into small pieces. Put it in a bowl of water and allow it to soak for several hours or overnight. This will loosen the fibers and begin the pulping process.

Step 2: Make a dipping screen by cutting the center out of a piece of Styrofoam. (The trays used to package fresh meat in the supermarket will work well.) Cut a piece of window screen to cover this opening and use duct tape to fasten it in place. You'll use this screen later to make sheets of paper; as you dip the screen into the pulpy water, the paper fibers will settle on the screen while the water flows right through.

Step 3: Put the paper pulp in the blender with plenty of water and grind it into a soupy paste. Add other ingredients (such as potpourri and coffee grounds) if desired.

Step 4: Pour the pulp into a dishpan half full of water. Make five or six more batches of pulp and add these too. The pulp will float.

Step 5: Slide your dipping screen under the floating pulp and lift it up so a thin layer of pulp coats the screen.

Step 6: Flip the screen over onto a damp towel and pat it lightly with a damp sponge so the pulp falls onto the towel. Lift off the screen.

Step 7: Next, fold the towel over the top of the pulp. Repeat this screening process until you have several sheets of pulp sandwiched between the towel. Use an additional towel if necessary.

Step 8: Put the towel and pulp "sandwiches" on the floor and place a piece of plywood on top. Stand on it to squeeze out the excess water.

Step 9: Peel back the towel and gently lift off the paper. Place each piece on a flat surface to dry overnight.

Step 10: To package handmade paper, place it in a pretty box, or use a thin satin ribbon to tie it against a piece of cardboard for stability.

Jewelry How-To's

Most women love jewelry, so it generally makes a great gift. The trick is to match the style of jewelry with the person. Refer back to your answers to the questionnaire in Chapter One to help focus in on someone's taste.

Safety Pin Bracelet

By combining safety pins with beads, you can create a unique bracelet in less than an hour. Use this simple technique to create a stretchable accessory to complement practically any outfit.

Step 1: Start with fifty-six No. 2 safety pins and at least two kinds of beads. Anything that fits on the pin can be used as an accent — beads, pearls, even tiny buttons and sequins. Just be sure the beads fit before you buy them.

Step 2: Leave half (twenty-eight) of the pins plain, and put beads on the other half. You can also vary the bead groupings; for instance, fourteen of one arrangement, and fourteen of another.

Step 3: Arrange the pins head to tail (every other one in opposite directions — see the illustration on page 107), always placing at least one plain pin between the beaded ones.

Step 4: Double a 36-inch length of elastic cord and thread it through one end of all the pins; then repeat on the opposite end. (You may want to use metallic elastic, sold in craft stores. For some designs, plain white elastic is fine.) Pull the cord ends together and knot them. Trim the excess cord. Hint: It's easier to thread the pins if you keep them flat on the table until both ends are threaded.

Step 5: You can also use this same technique to make necklaces. You can either use fifty-six pins as you did for the bracelet, and then string beads to fill out the rest of the necklace, or you can go for the powerful (and heavier!) statement of an entire necklace of pins.

Feather Earrings

Feather earrings make great gifts for women who love unique jewelry. The earrings can be subtle or flamboyant, depending on the feathers you use, but they're sure to have an exotic appeal that's irresistible.

Step 1: Choose at least two different kinds of feathers for each earring; contrasting textures and shapes are good. (Feathers are sold by the bag at craft shops and sporting goods stores — they're used for fly fishing.) Select individual feathers for each earring and arrange them on the table in front of you. Try to find feathers of similar size and shape for both earrings.

Step 2: If necessary, use scissors to trim the feathers to size. Large feathers, such as speckled goose secondaries, may need to be cut in half. Pull

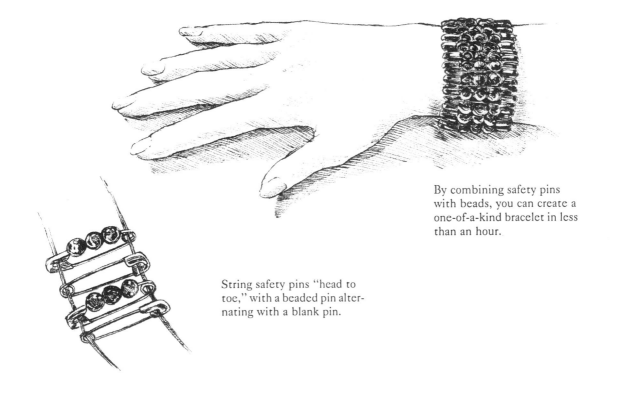

By combining safety pins with beads, you create a one-of-a-kind bracelet in less than an hour.

String safety pins "head to toe," with a beaded pin alternating with a blank pin.

off some filaments to expose the quills near the top (where the feather fits into the earring).

Step 3: Now, pinch or twist the feathers together at the top. (Use fine nylon thread to hold them securely, if you like.) Slip the ends of the feathers through the hole in an eye pin.

Step 4: Use three different beads for each earring, in colors that contrast or complement the feathers, for a total of six beads per pair. Holes should be big enough for the eye pins to pass through easily.

Thread three beads onto the eye pin, pulling them down snuggly over the quills. Then pull up the beads and put a dot of craft cement on the feathers. Push the beads back down to cover the quills.

Step 5: Grip the long end of the eye pin with the snipe nosed pliers directly above the beads. Twist the wire around the nose of one plier to form a loop. Snip off the excess wire with the tight fitting edge of the pliers (or use side cutting pliers). Pinch the cut end of the wire with the pliers so no sharp edges stick out; adjust the shape of the loop if necessary.

Step 6: To finish, put an earring wire through the loop. Repeat the same process to make the other earring.

Button Pin and Earring Set

Use buttons to make one-of-a-kind accessories in less than 5 minutes.

Step 1: To make a button pin, you'll need to find at least three buttons of varying sizes — large, medium and small. For the earrings, look for two identical buttons that coordinate in some way to the pin. If you have more buttons than you can use — or even if you know exactly which ones you'll be using, experiment with different arrangements for a little while. Look for relationships of color, texture, and size; try different combinations of buttons until you find your favorite. Consider both symmetrical and asymmetrical compositions before making a final decision.

Step 2: Some buttons have a projection ("shank") on the back for the thread to pass through. This shank must be removed to allow the button to lie flat. Some plastic shanks can be bitten off with pliers. (You need to squeeze the plastic so hard that it either crumbles or chips off.) For metal shanks, grasp the button firmly in one hand, and use the pliers to pull the shank out. Some all-metal buttons with

protruding shanks can be squeezed gently between the pliers to make them conform. Beware: Small plastic buttons may self-destruct when subjected to such rough treatment, although sometimes you might be able to glue them back together.

Step 3: Once the buttons lie flat in your arrangement, simply glue them in place. When this dries, glue the pin back on the opposite side. Be careful to place the pin slightly above center, so your brooch will hang correctly.

Step 4: You'll need at least two identical buttons to make the earrings. The simplest way to create a set is to use identical buttons — one on the pin and two more as earrings. But color is another effective way to pull it all together. Remove the shanks, if necessary, as you did for the pin. Then glue the earring post on the back and allow to dry.

Modeling Compound Jewelry

Modeling compound such as Fimo or Sculpey comes in a wide range of colors — or you can combine different colors to create your own unique hues. You can make earrings, pins and beads. Sketch out designs on paper, combining a large background shape with several smaller accent shapes. (Thanks to Tari Sasser Jacober for her input on these instructions. Look for the photo of her jewelry on page 95.)

Step 1: Cover your work surface with waxed paper. First you'll make your larger background shape. Cut a piece from a block of modeling compound and roll it out until it's slightly more than 1/16th of an inch thick. To make sure it's even, you may want to line up a couple of rulers to help contain the compound and keep it from getting spread too thin. (Tari says, "I cheat and put my Fimo through the noodle attachment of a pasta maker to avoid the hassle of trying to get a uniform thickness.") Cut two shapes such as triangles or squares, then set these aside.

Step 2: Make smaller shapes in a similar way. Roll out some of another color modeling compound, then cut out smaller shapes such as triangles or squares. You may also want to make little dots of a contrasting color by rolling tiny bits of compound between your fingers. Place them on the smaller shapes and set them aside.

Step 3: A typical way to work with modeling compound is to make stripes. These are called "caning."

Caning makes a good background for your other shapes. To make stripes, slice blocks of two different colors (purple and light blue, for instance) into four equal sections — 2 × 3-inch rectangles. Flatten them out slightly, and pile them on top of each other. Cut this rectangle in half, and put the second half on top, placing it so the colors continue to alternate. Then place a slice of another color on top (say, magenta) and slice the "sandwich" again, piling the new half on top. As an example, the order of the colors given would be as follows: purple, light blue, purple, light blue, magenta, light blue, purple, light blue, magenta, light blue, purple, etc. Continue until the pile is about an inch tall. You can then cut shapes out of the caning.

Step 4: Put together all your shapes — caning, large shapes and small — according to your design. Press slightly to bond. Put the assembled pin and earring shapes on a cookie sheet.

Step 5: To make beads, slice off a piece of caning and roll it up into a jelly roll. Run a darning needle across the bead in four different spots to create an interesting pattern. Pull these lines together at the end of the bead. Roll the bead lightly in your fingers

to smooth it out.

Step 6: To make the hole, stick your darning needle halfway into the bead and pull it out. Then stick it into the other end and push through to the first hole. This will prevent the hole from looking poked out on one side.

Step 7: Place your jewelry on a cookie sheet and bake for 15 minutes in a 225 degree oven. When the pieces have cooled thoroughly, glue on jewelry findings. Thread the beads onto a leather cord, visually center them; then tie knots to secure. Glue a jump ring and spring ring on opposite ends.

Paper Jewelry

You can make unique earrings, pins, and necklaces out of paper ribbon or watercolor paper. (Or use paper you've made yourself, as described on page 106.)

Step 1: To make shapes, cut poster board to size. Next, glue on paper ribbon, folding the excess to the back of the shape and mitering the corners. Or fold watercolor paper several times to make the desired shape, scoring the edges with a knife for nice clean lines.

To make fan-shaped earrings, accordian fold a 5-

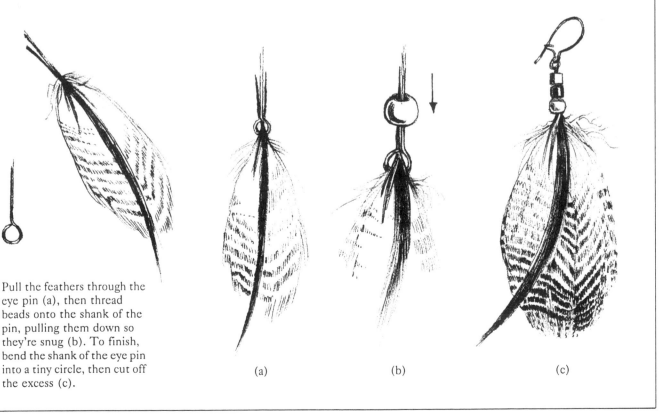

Pull the feathers through the eye pin (a), then thread beads onto the shank of the pin, pulling them down so they're snug (b). To finish, bend the shank of the eye pin into a tiny circle, then cut off the excess (c).

(a)   (b)   (c)

inch piece of paper or ribbon. The first and last fold should face the back. Pinch it together at the top to make a fan shape.

Step 2: If you use paper ribbon on cardboard, you may be ready to attach jewelry findings with hot glue at this point. If you're using watercolor paper, you may want to unfold your shape and cut small shapes with an X-Acto knife for visual interest before folding them up again. If you made fans, use an ice pick to punch a hole in the top. Attach jump rings and ear-wires.

Step 3: Use acrylic paints to make designs on the watercolor paper. Once dry, apply several coats of shellac and glue on findings.

FINISHING TOUCHES

*H*ow do you top a beautiful hand-made gift? With unique wrapping paper and a gift tag, that's how. An attractive package makes a gift even more appealing, and adds an extra special touch. Many years later, I still cherish a hand-painted tag my grandmother made one Christmas, though the gift itself is long forgotten. Most gift wrap ideas are simple enough for kids to do—and are a fun way for the family to spend some time together. In any case, making gift wrap is a relaxing, low stress way to express your creativity.

This chapter covers a variety of presentation possibilities that will give your gifts a special flair. Sometimes the gift itself will suggest a treatment. For example, a T-shirt printed with celery (see Chapter Four) might be wrapped in celery printed paper—if you use a large piece of scrap paper to practice on when you make the shirt, you may even be able to use this same paper to wrap the gift with! Gifts of jewelry are usually presented in small boxes; by decorating the box and lid separately, the recipient will be able to keep and use the box as well as the gift itself. Gift baskets are so pretty that you may want to simply encase them in semitransparent irridescent paper.

When looking for gift wrap possibilities, don't overlook old wrapping paper. My friend Lita is a consummate gift giver; she consistently creates special surprise packages that amaze the lucky recipient. She prides herself on recycling used wrapping paper, but no one would know unless she told them. Lita always gives her friends many small presents and at least one keynote, or large, gift. She collects all the gifts in a large box and wraps everything individually. Sometimes she tosses chocolate coins wrapped in foil in among the gaily wrapped boxes "to give prosperity."

Wrapping paper is the crowning glory of a gift. The following section lists some ideas to get you started, but as I've emphasized throughout this book, you're sure to think up some great ideas of your own.

IDEAS

Depending on the wrapping paper and the ribbon, flowers, novelties, or whatever you use to decorate with, you can create unusual designs that reflect the occasion, the season and the recipient's taste. Here are just a few ideas:

Rubber Stamps and More: With rubber stamps, stamp pads, colored pens, embossing powder, and glitter glue you can create unique handmade gift wraps and tags. (See some examples on page 99.) You'll find detailed instructions in the How-To section later in this chapter.

Collage Box: Kids love this technique, and I do too. If you make the lid separately, the package can be opened without damaging the collage, and the box can be used again. All you need to do is cut pictures out of old magazines and glue them onto a box. For instance, you can look for Christmasy pictures in old December issues of magazines and glue them onto a shoe box.

Sometimes a novelty or accessory can suggest a theme for a collage box, or be the finishing touch. I'd once completed a Christmas box featuring several pictures of teddy bears when I found a tiny teddy bear at a craft store. He went perfectly with the picture of the teddy bear on the lid, so I glued him onto the ribbon. Next time you're shopping for supplies, look for small gift accessories that might serve as the basis for a collage box.

Bag It: Most of us have more brown paper bags that we'd care to admit stashed in a closet or drawer. Here's a painless way to get rid of that excess paper and create goodwill at the same time. Draw a simple design on a piece of cardboard—seasonal themes such as hearts, jack o'lanterns, Christmas trees, holly, candles and Santa Claus are always good, or make a Southwestern or a floral design motif. Use a mat knife or an X-Acto to cut out your stencil, then place it on the flattened bag. (Iron the bags first, if they're crumpled.) Use a stencil brush or a sponge to apply paint within the cutout. Repeat until the side is finished; when this dries, repeat on the back. Add details with stamps, if you want. For instance, you can add ornaments to a Christmas tree by dipping the eraser end of a new pencil in red paint, then stamping with it. Top trees with stick-on gold stars, or cut a star out of sponge or potato and print it.

Elegant Gift Bags: Slightly more upscale than the Bag It idea, purchase plain gift bags with handles and then decorate them. These bags come in a wide range of colors; or you might be able to recycle a department store bag by painting over the store's logo.

Once your base coat dries, you can paint pictures, or print or stencil designs on the bag. Make coordinated gift tags and tie them onto the handle with ribbon.

Potpourri Package: This unique packaging idea, though not for everyone, is perfect for someone with a romantic or sensual nature, and anyone who loves good scents. Once the gift is wrapped, apply white craft glue liberally to the top of the package with a large brush, then sprinkle potpourri over the glue. Press the potpourri down gently; after 10 minutes, turn the package upside down and see what falls off. Make spot repairs as necessary; when these dry, tie the package with ribbon and a big bow.

A slightly more complicated version of the potpourri package has the advantage of letting the recipient reuse the potpourri. It involves buying a sheet of potpourri at the craft store, or making one yourself by sewing a large flat pouch out of lacy material, inserting potpourri, then sewing up the fourth side. Place this on top of the wrapped package, then secure it with ribbon and a bow.

Translucent Tissue Paper Effects: Cards and wrapping paper can be painted with wet tissue paper. First, use masking tape to outline the shape you want filled in on the card. Moisten colored tissue paper with water, and touch it lightly to the paper. Move the paper around to create patterns and shapes, then take it off and repeat with a different color. For more controlled designs, allow each color to dry before applying the next. Remove the masking tape once the card dries.

Colorful Paper Towel Wrap: You can make a lovely watercolor-look gift wrap using food coloring and paper towels. Mix at least twelve drops of each shade of food coloring with ¼ cup water in muffin tins. Fold or lightly crumple a paper towel, then dip the corners or edges into a color. Repeat this with other colors; then spread the towel flat on waxed paper to dry.

Faux Lace: Spray paint around paper doilies to create beautiful lacy effects on wrapping paper (and stationery, blank books, whatever). All you need to do is place doilies on your surface and spray lightly over them with paint. You may need to anchor the doilies down with small rocks to prevent them from blowing around in the paint spray. This paper looks great in combination with a tussie mussie, described next. Another idea is to simply glue the doilies themselves onto paper of a contrasting color.

Tussie Mussie: A great way to make wedding presents extra special is to wrap them with a special handmade paper, then top them with a small bouquet—a tussie mussie. (For instructions on how to make a tussie mussie, see page 37.) Place the tussie mussie on top of the wrapped package and tie it in place with excess ribbon from the wrappings. Use a round-headed decorative pin to secure the bouquet, if necessary. This treatment looks spectacular with the *faux* lace wrapping paper.

All that Glitters: Make jazzy gift wrap by squirting designs on freezer paper or aluminum foil with white glue, then sprinkling colored glitter over it. Let the paper lie flat until the glue dries, then pick it up and let the excess glitter fall onto another paper (so you can save the glitter and reuse it). Try making stripes, squiggles, circles, crosshatching, dots, lines or a random design. Tie with a metallic or reflective ribbon for an elegant package.

Celery Print Wrap: This dramatic-looking paper is a cinch to make. Simply cut off the end of a bunch of celery (save the stalks by standing them up in a glass of water and storing them in the refrigerator). Cover your work area with scrap paper before laying down the paper you're going to print. Use a paint brush to apply acrylic paint to the celery stump, then press it down firmly on your paper. I usually make several prints before repainting the celery, but if you want all the prints to be uniform, repaint it each time.

Note: Because wet paint interacts with tissue paper, it changes color after you apply it. In other words, you can use the same red paint and get totally different colors on yellow and green tissue paper. The colors are "organic," because they're interacting with the paper color, so they always look great. Also remember that tissue paper can be used as a liner inside the box, to cushion delicate presents or just for extra flair.

Potato-Printed Paper: Potatoes can be cut into a variety of shapes, then painted with a brush or simply dipped into paint, and stamped onto paper. By painting the same cut potato with different color combinations each time you stamp it, you multiply the effects. Potatoes can be cut into simple geometric shapes or carved into elaborate depictions of birds, flowers, mountains and more. See the How-To section of

Chapter Four (pages 57-60) for more details.

Sponge Printed Paper: Purchase either Miracle Sponges (which are thin and easy to cut) at a craft store, or ordinary kitchen sponges, then cut them into simple designs like hearts, flowers and birds, or geometric shapes like circles, squares and triangles. Dip the shapes into paint, then print with them on wrapping paper.

More Prints: You can print wrapping paper with leaves, burlap, feathers, sea sponges, flowers, broccoli, cabbage, oranges, onions, even finger or paw prints, if you have a docile pet. Look around the house for printing possibilities; and also check the How-To section of Chapter Three for advice.

Roller Wrappers: This technique is good if you have a large gift to wrap; it enables you to create an overall pattern in seconds flat. Simply tape waxed paper around a rolling pin, then glue string onto the waxed paper in pretty patterns. These could be simple lines, little flower shapes, or even crude animal shapes. Then wipe the rolling pin through some paint and roll it across your paper. Create visual interest by repeating the rolling process with another color once this dries.

Spatter Painted Paper: For an easy, attractive textural effect, try spatter painting (also called flyspecking) with a toothbrush. Put your paper in a cardboard box to contain the paint spray, dip an old toothbrush into paint, then flick the color onto the paper by rubbing over the bristles with your thumb. Use

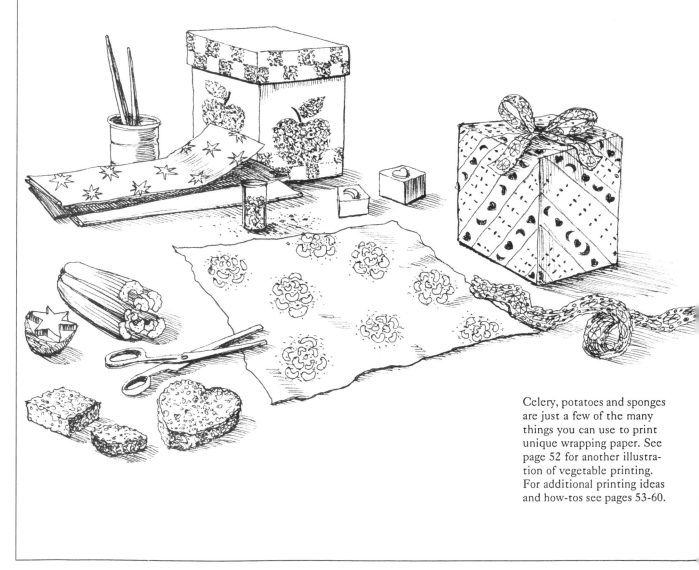

Celery, potatoes and sponges are just a few of the many things you can use to print unique wrapping paper. See page 52 for another illustration of vegetable printing. For additional printing ideas and how-tos see pages 53-60.

several different colors for interesting effects, or try white paint on black paper for a look that resembles the starry sky.

Special Finishes: Most of the special paint finishes described in Chapter Six can be used on wrapping paper. Ragging, combing, sponging, striating and mottling are especially pretty. Use several colors and play around with designs—also remember that sometimes practice paper from other projects can be called into service as wrapping paper.

Newspaper Recycling: Using newspaper as a wrapping recycles old paper that would otherwise be wasted, and it can look pretty, too. Just use colorful markers to make squiggles, lines, geometric motifs, or pictures on a sheet of newspaper to spice it up. Wrap the gift, then tie it with ribbon, yarn or embroidery floss that's color coordinated to the markings.

Novelties: Dimestore and craft novelties can make great gift wrapping accessories—things like little teddy bears, Christmas ornaments, small birds or paste fruit cost less than a dollar, but make a package stand out in a crowd. Tuck in a spray of pinecones or a couple of silk flowers; use them as is, or paint them gold for added drama. Sometimes you can find novelties that echo the gift, as my friend Sandy did for a housewarming gift. She was giving a gift to friends who had just closed on a house, so she glued little Monopoly game style houses on the ribbon.

Wrapping With Fabric: For gift wrap that lasts as long as the present itself, cover a bandbox (cardboard and papier-maché both work well) or other sturdy container with fabric. Floral chintz is a good fabric to use, but tailor your fabric choice to the recipient's taste. See page 117 for instructions; there's also a photo on page 116 and a color photo on page 47.

Fabric Cards: When giving gifts you've sewn, or when using fabric-wrapped boxes, use a scrap of fabric to make a card. Dip the scraps in white glue thinned with a little water. Let them dry on a sheet of waxed paper, then press out wrinkles with your fingers. Cut out shapes, then glue them onto heavy paper to make cards.

Handmade Paper: For small gifts, handmade paper can be a unique wrapping material. Use colored paper scraps to make your pulp, or just use the natural color for an organic look; see the How-To section of Chapter Six, page 106, for instructions on paper making. Tie your package up with a cloth ribbon (grosgrain or satin) or twine.

Calendar Gift Wrap: If you're one of those people who can't bear to part with old calendars because of the pretty pictures, put them to good use as wrapping paper. Tie with a color coordinated ribbon for an utterly unique package.

Tarjetaria: This Latin American technique (pronounced tar-het-air-EE-ah) uses embossing to create keepsake cards. Using a special burnisher, you create raised lettering and designs similar to the fancy custom stationery that must be special ordered through a printer. Each card is unique, and looks fantastic. Tarjetaria is easy to do—all you need are vellum paper, colored pens and a ball-tipped burnisher for pressing your designs into the paper. These supplies are sold at art supply stores; see the How-To section for instructions.

Batik or Painted Silk Cards: Use the techniques described in Chapter Four to make small designs on scraps of cloth that can then be glued onto heavy bond paper, and folded into card shapes.

Magazine Gift Cards: Cut pictures of artwork or beautiful landscapes out of magazines and rubber cement them onto heavy paper or card stock. *New Yorker* cartoons make great comical tags; I once saved a "Peanuts" cartoon about Father's Day until the next year and made a card out of it for my dad.

Christmas Tags: This is similar to the magazine card idea, but uses last year's Christmas cards to make gift tags for packages. Simply cut the backs off (where the card was signed) and use the picture on the front as a tag.

Inner Workings: Make your gift box special to open by tucking potpourri, confetti or streamers inside the tissue paper liner. Or, nest the gift in printed paper or shredded colored paper inside the box for a dramatic presentation.

Raveled Ribbons: You probably know you can curl ribbons using the side of a scissors, but you can also ravel them for a unique, festive look. Gently pull apart the ribbons lengthwise so they separate into strands, then curl them using the side of a scissors. This decorative technique looks really festive when you use different colors of ribbon on the same package. (If you really like the way this looks, invest in a ribbon shredder, sold at craft stores and gift shops.)

In the Mail: If a gift must be mailed, wrap it before putting in another box for sending. Then use the colored comics pages from Sunday papers, colorful tissue paper, or pages ripped from magazines to stuff around the sides of the gift as insulation. This makes for a colorful surprise when the recipient opens the box.

HOW-TO'S

For how-to instructions on various printing techniques, see Chapter Four; for special finishes, see Chapter Six.

Stamped Gift Wrap and Tags

Using ink, rubber stamps, embossing powder, felt pens and glitter glue, you can make beautiful holiday gift wraps. Supplies are available at craft stores or from the Personal Stamp Exchange, 345 S. McDowell Blvd. #342, Petaluma, CA 94952; (707)763-8058.

Step 1: For basic stamped paper, ink your stamp thoroughly on the stamp pad, then press it down firmly on the paper. Re-ink each time you stamp. Work first with one color ink, leaving blank spots for your second pass with another color, if desired.

Step 2: To make extra special gift wraps, use embossing ink. Pour clear embossing ink from the bottle onto a blank pad; ink your stamp on this pad then press it firmly onto the paper. Repeat four or five times before sprinkling with colored embossing powder. (The powder sticks to the areas that have been stamped, so work quickly before the ink dries.)

Next, either shake or brush off the excess powder, then hold the image over the hot plate until the powder has melted completely — it will then harden into a raised, embossed design. Repeat this process, working with four or five images at one time, until the paper is covered. Then fill in details with a brush pen or felt-tip pen, and add highlights with Glitter Glue.

Step 3: To make a matching tag, use a *To: From:* stamp on a small piece of card stock. Decorate it using one of the procedures from Step 2. Glue this card onto a slightly larger card of a contrasting color. Poke a hole in the upper left hand corner with an awl or darning needle, then tie on a ribbon that can be used to attach the card to the gift.

Presenting potpourri in a fabric-wrapped box helps make this simple gift extra special.

Fabric-Covered Boxes

Doubling as storage containers as well as packages for gifts, these beautiful boxes live on after the gift-giving occasion has passed. Bandboxes (hatboxes) are especially pretty, but any round lidded box will work.

Step 1: Place the box at the edge of your fabric; use a pencil to mark this spot on the inside of the box. This will be your starting point. Now, measure the fabric by rolling the box over it, overlapping your starting point by an inch. Add an inch to the top edge, and ¼ inch to the bottom edge. Cut the fabric. Fold under the ¼ inch at the bottom and press; glue it into place.

Step 2: To make fabric shapes for the lid and bottom of the box, trace the lid shape onto the wrong side of the fabric; then add ¼ inch extra all around. Cut this out, then repeat, so you have two circles.

Step 3: To trim the edge of the box lid, cut the same length of fabric as you did for the box shape. Use the width of the lid, plus ¼ inch extra on both sides. Press these ¼-inch edges under and glue them into place.

Step 4: Cover the top of the lid with white glue,

smoothing it out with a paintbrush to eliminate air bubbles and bumps. Place the fabric on the lid and rub it down with your fingers. Cut small notches in the edge of the overhanging fabric so it will lie flat, then glue it to the sides of the lid. Repeat this procedure for the bottom of the box.

Step 5: Brush glue on the sides of the lid, smooth it out, then carefully place your trim piece, with both edges folded under, on the lid. Press firmly in place.

Step 6: Apply white glue to the box itself, then smooth it out. Place the fabric on your box, lining up the finished (glued hem) edge with the bottom. Rub it in place with your fingers. Then fold the overhang fabric over the top edge of the box and glue it down inside.

Tarjetaria

Tarjeta in Spanish means "card" or "label," the suffix signifies "to make." This Latin American card making technique (pronounced tar-het-air-EE-ah) uses a special burnisher to emboss raised designs onto vellum cards. This special, semitransparent paper is strong and stretches instead of tearing; it looks white

The wire hanger makes it easy to attach the finished bow to your package.

and opaque where it's been burnished. Use tarjetaria to create your own professional-looking cards that are custom-made for the recipient. The special supplies you'll need (the burnisher, rubber burnishing pad, and vellum paper) are available from Artemus & Co., 30-22 10th St., Villa Carolina, Carolina, Puerto Rico 00630; (809)768-6535.

Step 1: Plan your entire design on a piece of scrap paper, including wording. Once you've perfected your idea, make an enclosure card by folding your vellum tracing paper in half. Unfold it, then place it right side up on top of your design. Hold the vellum in place with masking tape so it doesn't slip.

Step 2: Use a fine-tipped marker to trace your design onto the front half of the vellum. Hold your pen at a 90-degree angle for a smooth line.

Step 3: Once dry, turn the inked card over and used colored markers to fill in the design on the back of the card.

Step 4: Now, practice burnishing the design on a piece of scrap vellum. To do this, lay the paper face down on the rubber burnishing pad. Hold the burnisher like a pencil and press firmly against the paper, tracing the lines of the design. Add highlights by stroking the paper with the burnisher as if with a paint brush. Burnish the edges of the card by placing a ruler along the straight edge of the card and pulling the burnisher against the ruler.

Step 5: When you're comfortable with the technique, burnish your card, choosing elements of the design you wish to play up.

Step 6: An optional step highlights the card with color shading using oil pastels. Turn the card wrong side up. Load a small amount of oil pastel on a cotton swab, choosing a color that will complement the inner card you'll be adding in Step Seven. Rub the color evenly around the design using a small circular motion.

Step 7: Make an inner card out of a coordinating color of bond paper. Fold the paper in half and place it inside the vellum card with the folds together. Run a glue stick across the top of the fold, then press in place so the cards will stick together.

Ribbons and Bows

The final touch that makes a gift look really spectacular is a big bow. Here are some simple instructions for making two different kinds.

Bow Method No. 1

Step 1: Start with a 2-foot length of ribbon; make a loop at one end. Make another loop to form a bow shape, keeping the ribbon right side out. The loops should be the same size.

Step 2: Loop the long piece of ribbon over the front of the bow to form a third loop, then double it back to make a fourth. Always keep the ribbon right side out. You can repeat this process once or twice again to make a fuller bow if you want.

Step 3: Wrap a piece of florist wire around the center of the bow and twist it to hold the bow in place. Trim the ends. Take a small piece of ribbon and wrap it over the wire to camouflage it; hold this in place with a dot of glue on the back, where the ends come together. Use the wire to fasten the bow onto the ribbon wrapped around the package; then trim the excess wire.

Bow Method No. 2

Step 1: Wrap a piece of ribbon around your hand five times, making sure the ribbon is lined up in one continuous loop. If you're using cloth ribbon, take a small stitch with needle and thread to connect the end of the ribbon to the loop next to it, so it stays in place. (Use tape if you're working with paper ribbon.) Slide the ribbon off your fingers, keeping the loop intact.

Step 2: Fold the loop in half, and cut small triangles out of the center of both sides of the doubled loop, as shown in the illustration on page 119. Be sure the triangles don't meet, or your bow will be ruined!

Step 3: Tie the ribbon together at the triangles with a new piece of ribbon; pull the loops out carefully one at a time. Twist them gently as you pull. Tie the bow onto the package with excess ribbon from the wrapping.

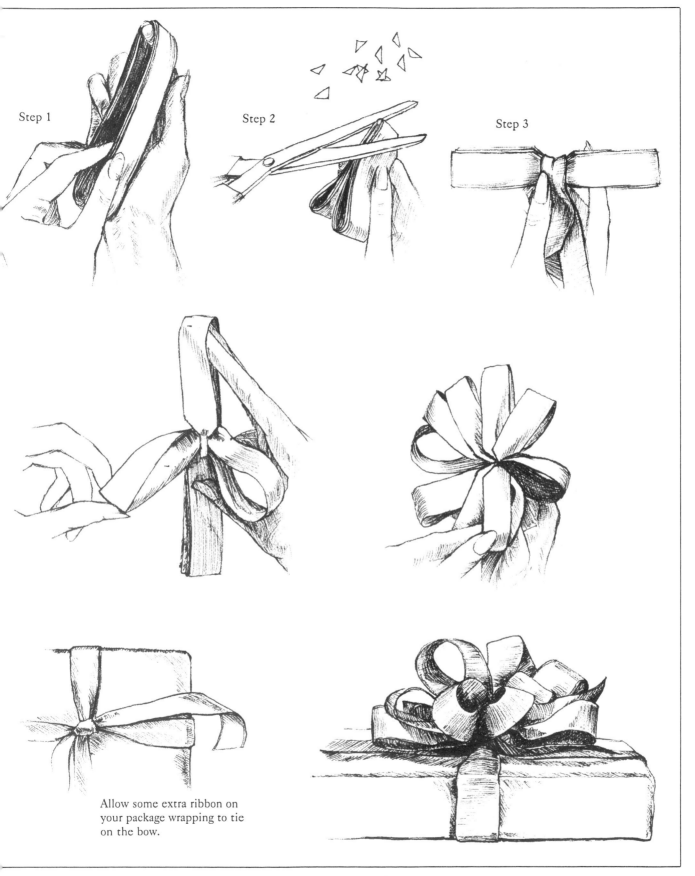

Step 1

Step 2

Step 3

Allow some extra ribbon on
your package wrapping to tie
on the bow.

INDEX

AFTERWORD

In the course of reading this book, I hope you found gift ideas for everyone on your list. You may have come up with some great ideas of your own. If you want to share them, feel free to write me at the following address:

Beth Franks
% North Light Books
1507 Dana Avenue
Cincinnati, OH 45207